The **HTML Pocket**Guide

BruceHyslop

W0009621

Ginormous knowledge, pocket-sized.

**Peachpit
Press**

The HTML Pocket Guide
Bruce Hyslop

Peachpit Press
1249 Eighth Street
Berkeley, CA 94710
510/524-2178
510/524-2221 (fax)

Find us on the Web at: www.peachpit.com
To report errors, please send a note to: errata@peachpit.com

Peachpit Press is a division of Pearson Education.

Executive Editor: Clifford Colby
Editor: Kim Wimpsett
Technical Editor: Michael Bester
Production Editor: Tracey Croom
Compositor: David Van Ness
Indexer: James Minkin
Cover Design: Peachpit Press
Interior Design: Peachpit Press

ISBN-13:   978-0-321-69974-9
ISBN-10:   0-321-69974-2

9 8 7 6 5 4 3 2 1

Printed and bound in the United States of America

To Mom and Dad, and your nearly 45 years of marriage.

To Merri, my birthday mate; you are greatly missed.

About the Author

Bruce Hyslop has 13 years of experience in Web development, with a focus on interface technical architecture and development. He is the senior director of the Interface Engineering Group (IEG) at Schematic, an interactive agency based in the United States. In this role, Bruce oversees companywide efforts to define and implement best practices regarding HTML, CSS, JavaScript, and accessibility wherever they may be applied: the browser, desktop, mobile devices, and emerging platforms.

An early adopter of Web standards, Bruce has helmed IEG for more than 120 projects, including clients such as ABC, BBC, Dell, Logitech, Microsoft, NBC Universal, Nokia, and Target, among others. In addition to his development and writing efforts, Bruce teaches a CSS course at UCLA Extension.

Acknowledgments

First I'd like to say a very grateful thank you to Nancy Davis and Cliff Colby for the opportunity and for your continued patience and support, of which I'm very appreciative.

A most sincere thank-you goes out to Nicole Neopolitan and Patrick Ty. I could not possibly have done this without your support.

Thank you, Kim and Michael, for all your editing suggestions and improvements and for catching my errors. It was always very comforting to know you'd be reviewing my words with care and experienced eyes.

Thank you, Charlene Will, Tracey Croom, Cory Borman, and David Van Ness, for taking great care in the design and being such a pleasure with which to work.

Thank you, James Minkin, (from me and on behalf of our readers!) for indexing the content .

Thank you, everyone at Peachpit with whom I didn't have an opportunity to work with directly but who contributed to the book's efforts and will continue to do so.

Thank you to my fellow IEGers at Schematic for their continued inspiration, and to Michael Roldan, Tommy Ly, Karen Lauritsen, Scott Hutchinson, and Robert Reinhardt.

Last, but certainly not least, a special acknowledgment to those of you who were particularly neglected while I wrote this. You often inspired me in quiet but profound ways. I have a lot of catching up to do!

Contents

Introduction

Welcome to the *HTML Pocket Guide*! I'm excited you're here.

HTML—the humble markup language that helped spur a new era of information sharing two decades ago—is hotter than ever today with the emergence of HTML5. So, now is a great time to either learn about HTML for the first time or be sure you're on top of the latest developments.

In this introduction, I summarize what you can expect to learn, whom the book targets, how information is presented, and where you can learn more.

What You Will Learn

The focus of this book is to help you learn about

- Elements and attributes in HTML 4, XHTML 1, and HTML5

- Differences between these HTML versions

- Current Web standards–based best practices regarding HTML usage

- What to use instead of deprecated attributes

Who This Book Is For

This book is suitable for developers and designers of all skill levels who want to learn about HTML and for those who want a handy, informative HTML reference at the ready. Those of you who have X/HTML down pat will be interested in its detailed coverage of all the HTML5 elements.

How to Read This Book

This book is structured to allow you to read it either sequentially (especially Parts 2 and 3) or jump to a particular topic for quick access to specific answers. The book has three parts:

- Part 1 covers an HTML5 overview, HTML fundamentals, and common attributes and data types referred to by Parts 2 and 3.

- Part 2 provides in-depth coverage of all HTML elements and their attributes except those unique to HTML5. It also explains differences for some of these elements when used in HTML5. All of this information is in a reference-style format that includes code examples and explanations concerning how and when to use the elements and attributes.

- Part 3 has the same format, except it focuses on elements unique to HTML5. In that sense, it's like a book within the book, which is especially convenient if your main goal is to get up to speed on the new elements in HTML5.

Support Site

I have also created a support site that will continue to grow after the book's release. It's located at *http://www.htmlfiver.com/html-pocket-guide/* and includes additional coverage, code examples, a list of the links referenced in the book, and errata. Among the code examples are several sample HTML templates that demonstrate how to use a variety of the elements described in Parts 2 and 3 together in completed pages. I also welcome feedback so we can make the next version of the book even better.

Conventions Used in This Book

This book uses several conventions for the code, attributes, and terminology.

Code

Most code examples follow XHTML Strict syntax (which is appropriate both for XHTML and for HTML5), with the occasional example in Part 3 including unterminated empty elements to demonstrate HTML5's flexibility. (Please see "An HTML5 Overview" in Chapter 1.)

Inline code and code blocks share the same font treatment; portions particularly requiring your attention are highlighted. An arrow indicates code that is wrapped for display purposes at an "unnatural" point and that you should type on a single line in your HTML instead.

Example:

```
<p>Oooooh, I want to ride on <a href="http://en.wikipedia.
➥ org/wiki/File:Whalom_comet_enter.jpg" title="Flyer Comet">
➥ <em>that</em> roller coaster</a>!</p>
```

Code rendered in a browser, when not shown with a screen shot, appears like this:

Oooooh, I want to ride on *that* roller coaster!

Attributes

I indicate an element's attributes in a particular manner throughout the book. Please see "How Attributes Are Noted in This Book" in Chapter 1 for details.

Terminology

I use these terms throughout the book:

- *HTML* refers to the markup language in general, covering HTML 4.01, XHTML 1, HTML5, and XHTML5.

- *HTML 4* refers to HTML 4.01.

- *XHTML* refers to XHTML 1.

- *X/HTML* refers to both HTML 4.01 and XHTML 1. (You'll often see this represented as *(X)HTML* in other resources.)

- *HTML5* refers to HTML5 (and with a nod to XHTML5), specifically the HTML5 Working Draft of April 26, 2010, that is still under development at the time of this writing.

- *User agent* and *browser* are used mostly interchangeably; though, technically, a browser is a user agent, the reverse isn't necessarily true (for instance, screen readers and search engine spiders are also user agents).

- In the context of HTML, *document* means the same thing as *page* (such as, "When the browser loads the page . . ."). It's just a more formal term.

I hope you enjoy the book!

Part 1

HTML Basics

This part of the book contains one chapter, "HTML Basics," which provides an overview of HTML5, discusses the versions of HTML, recommends some best practices, lists common attributes, and more.

Part 1 Contents

HTML Basics

This chapter provides foundational information for Parts 2 and 3 of the book. (If you've been around HTML for awhile, much of it will be old hat.)

I cover a few standards-based best practices, basic HTML document structure for all flavors of the language (including HTML5), differences among the versions, DOCTYPEs, basic data types, common attributes, a note about obsolete and deprecated items, and more.

note I encourage all readers to review the "How Attributes Are Noted in This Book" box.

Let's begin with an overview of HTML5 in case this version of HTML is new to you.

An HTML5 Overview

HTML5 is a natural evolution of HTML 4 that accounts for the rapid growth of media, rich online experiences, and sophisticated Web application development since HTML 4.01 became a specification at the end of 1999.

At the time of this writing, HTML5 is still under development and subject to change. However, it is on stable footing, and browsers have already added many—and continue to add more—of its features. (Please see *http://www.htmlfiver.com/html5-browser-support/* for more information.)

This book includes information from the HTML5 editor's Working Draft dated April 26, 2010. Here are some key links so you can keep up with HTML5's progress:

- **W3C Working Draft**: *http://www.w3.org/TR/html5/*.

- **Latest editor's Working Draft (typically more recent)**: *http://www.whatwg.org/specs/web-apps/current-work/multipage/*.

- **HTML, The Markup Language**: *http://www.w3.org/TR/html-markup/*. This briefly summarizes each HTML5 element and attribute.

- **HTML5 differences from HTML4**: *http://www.w3.org/TR/html5-diff/*.

Snapshot View

HTML5 breaks down like this:

- **New elements and attributes**: HTML5 inherits nearly every element from HTML 4 (please see Part 2 of the book). It also includes nearly 30 new elements, all of which I detail in Part 3 of the book. Highlights include audio, video, canvas, datalist, and a whole host of new semantics such as article, nav, header, and footer. As discussed in Chapter 7, HTML5 also includes big advancements in the forms department with new attributes and input types that make rich forms easier to develop, more accessible, and more consistent for users and that can validate in the browser without JavaScript.

- **New features**: *Features* is a bit of a broad term, but it mostly speaks to new functionality in HTML5 and related in-progress specs that fall under HTML5 from a "marketing" sense, if not literally part of HTML5. (Aside from the occasional coverage, this book leaves in-depth discussions of the new features for another day.) Some of these features are:
  - Canvas (via the aforementioned canvas element)
  - Cross-document messaging
  - Drag and drop
  - Embedding of Scalable Vector Graphics (SVG) directly in HTML
  - Geolocation
  - History (browser) management
  - Microdata
  - Native media playback scripting (via the aforementioned audio and video elements)
  - Offline Web Applications
  - Web Storage (aka DOM storage)
  - Web Workers

Code Formatting Syntax: A Recommendation

HTML5 is extremely forgiving concerning how you may structure the code. You may include or omit closing tags, use uppercase or lowercase elements and attributes, quote or not quote attribute values, and more. That flexibility has been the source of some controversy, but it remains.

Having said that, **my recommendation** is to code HTML5 in either one of these two ways:

- Use all lowercase for code, double-quote all attribute values, use attribute minimization, always use an element's end tag if it has one, and don't terminate elements that don't have an end tag (that is, empty or void elements).

- Or, use XHTML syntax, which is exactly the same as the previous bullet, except you don't use attribute minimization and *do* terminate empty elements. Yes, HTML5 accepts XHTML syntax.

All the code examples in this book conform to one of these (mostly the second) so you can get a sense of how to replicate them if you're new to coding. (Please see "Differences Between HTML 4 and XHTML" later in this chapter for explanations of attribute minimization and terminating empty elements. Their descriptions are relevant to HTML5 usage, too.)

> **note** Why do I recommend following one of these formats? I elaborate a bit on this at *http://www.htmlfiver.com/extras/html5-code-syntax/*, but the short answer is they're in line with the way seasoned developers and designers have coded for the better part of the past decade as a result of the Web standards movement. So, these syntax formats will become de facto HTML5 coding standards, in my view, if they aren't already.

> **note** Unlike HTML5, XHTML5 syntax *does* have firm rules, just like XHTML 1. However, unlike XHTML 1, an XHTML5 page must be *served* with an XML MIME type, and if there is a single invalid portion of code, the page won't render. For this reason, HTML5 will have widespread use, while XHTML5 will likely find a limited audience.

How to Style New Elements

Although it's true that you can't use HTML5 features such as the additional input types and the details element unless a browser supports their behavior, you can use the new semantic elements such as article, aside, nav and most of the others right away. Plus, with just a little extra help, most browsers allow you to style them even when they don't yet support them natively. I've detailed the three easy steps required to style these elements at http://www.htmlfiver.com/extras/style-html5-elements/.

So, that's a bird's eye view of HTML5. Please dig into Parts 2 and 3 to learn the nitty-gritty concerning HTML5 element usage, and visit *http://www.htmlfiver.com/using-html5-today/* to learn more about what you can use in HTML5 today.

A Few Best Practices

I could easily dedicate chapters to Web standards and best practices but have synthesized them into these key points:

- **Always use a DOCTYPE**: A DOCTYPE tells the browser what mode in which to render, improves interoperability, and makes your life a heck of a lot easier when developing and debugging your code. Please see the "DOCTYPEs" section for more information.

- **Separate content, presentation, and behavior**: Along with the next item, this is one of *the* key tenets of Web standards. Separation of content (HTML), presentation (CSS), and behavior (JavaScript) means not intermingling them in the HTML. Usually it's best to place your CSS and JavaScript in separate files and load them into your pages. Among other benefits, this makes development, reusability, and maintenance far easier. (Make one CSS or JavaScript update, and it can spill across your whole site.)

- **Use proper semantics**: This refers to wrapping your content with the HTML element(s) that best reflects the nature of the content. For example, put each paragraph of text in a paragraph element (<p></p>). Place a list of items in a definition list (<dl></dl>), ordered list (<ol></ol>), or unordered list (<ul></ul>) as is most appropriate; it's the same principle for other types of content and their related elements. This improves accessibility, improves search engine optimization (SEO), tends to make pages lighter, and usually makes styling with CSS easier as well.

- **Validate your pages**: HTML validators check your code for syntax errors. By validating your pages, you'll be sure they're in compliance with their DOCTYPE. This helps you create more consistent code and track down the occasional nettlesome bug. Validate your X/HTML pages at *http://validator.w3.org/* and your HTML5 pages there or at *http://html5.validator.nu/* to receive the kind of personal validation and satisfaction that only an automated program can provide!

Basic HTML Document Structure

No matter what flavor of HTML you're writing—HTML 4, XHTML 1, or HTML5—the basic structure remains the same. Only a few of the details are different. Let's take a look.

Example 1 (a typical XHTML 1 Strict page):

```
<!DOCTYPE html PUBLIC "-//W3C//DTD XHTML 1.0 Strict//EN"
    "http://www.w3.org/TR/xhtml1/DTD/xhtml1-strict.dtd">
<html xmlns="http://www.w3.org/1999/xhtml" xml:lang="en"
lang="en">
<head>
    <title>Your document title</title>
    <meta http-equiv="Content-type" content="text/html;
charset=utf-8" />
</head>
<body>
    . . . [your page content] . . .
```

```
</body>
</html>
```

I've highlighted the portions that change from one version of the language to another. They are as follows:

- **The DOCTYPE**: Include a DOCTYPE in every page. See the "DOCTYPEs" section in this chapter for more information, including a list of available DOCTYPEs.

- **The html element**: This is simply `<html lang="en">` for HTML 4 and HTML5 documents, where `lang` is customized accordingly to fit the language of your page content. (Please see "Language Codes" in this chapter.) English is specified in the example.

- **The meta element that includes the character encoding**: An HTML 4 document doesn't have the trailing slash (`/>`). An HTML5 document may have the trailing slash if you'd like but is otherwise simplified to `<meta charset="utf-8">`, assuming the encoding is UTF-8. It's also preferable to put it before the `title`. (See the `meta` element in Chapter 3.)

For comparison, Example 2 shows a typical HTML5 document.

Example 2:

```
<!DOCTYPE html>
<html lang="en">
<head>
    <meta charset="utf-8" />
    <title>Your document title</title>
</head>
<body>
    . . . [your page content] . . .
</body>
</html>
```

Differences Between HTML 4 and XHTML

In addition to the basic structural differences just discussed, there are a number of other differences between HTML 4 and XHTML 1 (they're true of XHTML5, too). They're all easy to get a handle on; this section of the XHTML 1 spec summarizes them nicely: *http://www.w3.org/TR/xhtml1/#diffs*.

I do want to call out two of the key differences, though, since you'll come across them frequently in Parts 2 and 3 of the book:

- **Terminate empty elements**: Some elements are classified as empty elements (also called *void*). An empty element is one that can't contain content, so it doesn't have an end tag. Examples are <img> and <br>. In XHTML, empty elements must be self-closing, which is simply a matter of ending them with />, as in <img /> and <br />. Most of my code samples throughout the book use XHTML syntax (which is also valid in HTML5), but you will see notes such as "<area> or <area />" in the summary of relevant elements as a reminder of the two formats.

- **An attribute must have a value (even Booleans)**: Some attributes don't have a value, like the selected attribute on <option selected></option>. This syntax is referred to as *attribute minimization*. Most of these are *Boolean attributes*, meaning that if they are present, the condition is true (the option is selected), and if they aren't, it is false. XHTML documents don't allow attribute minimization, so you simply assign the name of the attribute as the attribute value, making the example become <option selected="selected"></option>. (Note that HTML5 allows either selected, selected="", or selected="selected", all of which browsers should treat the same way.)

 Please also see "Code Formatting Syntax: A Recommendation" earlier in this chapter.

Differences Between HTML 4 and HTML5

Some elements are different when used in HTML 4 or XHTML 1 documents versus in HTML5. I detail these differences throughout Part 2 of the book. Please see the introduction to Part 2 regarding how I typically convey that information. I also recommend you refer to the handy W3C summary at *http://www.w3.org/TR/html5-diff/*.

 Please also see "Code Formatting Syntax: A Recommendation" earlier in this chapter.

DOCTYPEs

HTML comes in a few flavors, as dictated by a page's DOCTYPE (always include one in your documents!). This section includes a reference of the available DOCTYPES and a brief summary of what each allows.

Standards-savvy developers and designers have tended to use XHTML 1 Strict or Transitional and, in some cases, HTML 4.01 Strict. However, you can use the HTML5 DOCTYPE today, and your pages will work as expected (that doesn't mean all of HTML5's new elements will work since that depends on the browser, but you can code your pages as you normally would otherwise).

HTML 4.01 Strict

```
<!DOCTYPE HTML PUBLIC "-//W3C//DTD HTML 4.01//EN"
"http://www.w3.org/TR/html4/strict.dtd">
```

Deprecated elements and attributes, frames, and the target attribute on links are not allowed.

HTML 4.01 Transitional (aka Loose)

```
<!DOCTYPE HTML PUBLIC "-//W3C//DTD HTML 4.01 Transitional//EN"
"http://www.w3.org/TR/html4/loose.dtd">
```

Deprecated elements and attributes are allowed.

HTML 4.01 Frameset

```
<!DOCTYPE HTML PUBLIC "-//W3C//DTD HTML 4.01 Frameset//EN"
"http://www.w3.org/TR/html4/frameset.dtd">
```

A variant of HTML 4.01 Transitional that is used for frames only.

HTML5 and XHTML5

```
<!DOCTYPE html>
```

Used for all HTML5 documents.

XHTML 1 Strict

```
<!DOCTYPE html PUBLIC "-//W3C//DTD XHTML 1.0 Strict//EN"
"http://www.w3.org/TR/xhtml1/DTD/xhtml1-strict.dtd">
```

You must follow XHTML syntax rules; plus, deprecated elements and
attributes, frames, and the target attribute on links are not allowed.

XHTML 1 Transitional

```
<!DOCTYPE html PUBLIC "-//W3C//DTD XHTML 1.0 Transitional//EN"
"http://www.w3.org/TR/xhtml1/DTD/xhtml1-transitional.dtd">
```

You must follow XHTML syntax rules. Deprecated elements and attributes are allowed.

XHTML 1 Frameset

```
<!DOCTYPE html PUBLIC "-//W3C//DTD XHTML 1.0 Frameset//EN"
"http://www.w3.org/TR/xhtml1/DTD/xhtml1-frameset.dtd">
```

A variant of XHTML 1 Transitional used for frames only.

XHTML 1.1

```
<!DOCTYPE html PUBLIC "-//W3C//DTD XHTML 1.1//EN"
"http://www.w3.org/TR/xhtml11/DTD/xhtml11.dtd">
```

Equal to XHTML 1 Strict but allows you to include additional modules.

Inline vs. Block-level Elements

A *block-level* element may contain most other block-level elements and all inline elements. *Inline* elements mostly describe brief strings of text and may include other inline elements. For instance, the p element is a block-level element, and the em element is inline: `<p>This is a <em>great</em> example!</p>`. Block-level elements occupy at least one full line when rendering, while inline elements take up only as much space as their content requires. This default behavior may be overridden with the CSS display property.

HTML5 doesn't use the terms *block-level* and *inline*, though its elements do render by default in one of the two ways. Please see "Content models" at *http://www.w3.org/TR/html5/dom.html#content-models* for details.

HTML Comments

HTML comments don't render in the page, just in the code. They must start with `<!--` and end with `-->` and they may cover several lines of code. I recommend commenting at least the beginning and end of major sections of your pages to make your code easier to read.

Attributes

An HTML element's attribute defines a property of that element. They are optional in most cases, so use them only as needed. For example, here you see both the href and title attributes applied to a hyperlink:

```
<p>They saw a <a href="ducks.html" title="Essay and
photos">family of ducks</a> by the stream.</p>
```

You may place attributes in any order you like, but I encourage you to be consistent in your approach in order to make your code easier to read and manage.

I'll detail common attributes in just a bit, but first please indulge me as I explain how attributes are noted in this book.

How Attributes Are Noted in This Book

Many HTML elements share the same attributes. The X/HTML specifications use the terms *Core*, *I18n*, and *Events* to categorize these. (Core consists of mostly unrelated common attributes, I18n consists of the internationalization-related attributes, and Events are the event-related attributes.) Meanwhile, HTML5 uses one term only, *Global*, which represents all the Core, I18n, and Events attributes from X/HTML *plus* a bunch just for HTML5. (I explain each of these attribute groupings in detail after this box.)

I use these terms throughout Parts 2 and 3 of the book. Namely, the beginning of each HTML element entry includes a list of its attributes in this format:

Attributes Core, I18n, Events, accesskey, alt, href, nohref*, shape,
HTML5 Only: Global, hreflang, media, ping

(continues on next page)

How Attributes Are Noted
in This Book (continued)

An "Attributes in Detail" section that details their usage appears toward the end of an HTML element's entry.

So, in this example, the element supports all the Core, I18n, Events, and (in HTML5 only) Global attributes. In addition, the attributes listed by name (accesskey, alt, href, nohref*, shape, hreflang, media, and ping) are custom attributes that the element supports, depending on the version of HTML. In case it's not clear, all attributes prior to *HTML5 Only* apply to HTML 4, XHTML 1, *and* HTML5 (except when noted otherwise in "Attributes in Detail"), and all attributes after *HTML5 Only* apply to HTML5 only, as you would expect.

If an attribute has an asterisk, as nohref does in the example, then that indicates an exception is noted in "Attributes in Detail." For instance, it might say this: nohref: *Obsolete in HTML5.*

note The accesskey and tabindex attributes are shared by a handful of elements in X/HTML though are not part of the Core, I18n, or Events attribute groupings. They *are* part of HTML5's Global attributes, though, so please find their descriptions in that section. The same definitions apply to their use in X/HTML documents.

OK, let's look at the attribute groupings.

Core

These attributes are both part of X/HTML's Core group and HTML5's Global group of common attributes:

- class="*class names*": Use this to assign one or more space-separated class names to an element for styling or scripting purposes. You may

define your own class names, such as `<p class="news synopsis">`. . .
`</p>`. A class may be repeated in a page, whether it's to the same or
different element types.

- `id="`*unique identifier*`"`: This assigns a unique ID for functional, styling,
  and scripting purposes. It may not be repeated within the same page.

- `style="`*inline style sheet*`"`: This assigns inline CSS to an element. Avoid
  using this whenever possible since it is a best practice not to mix your
  presentation (CSS) and content (HTML).

- `title="`*descriptive text*`"`: This provides a short description that doesn't
  appear on-screen, though most browsers render it as a tooltip when
  the mouse or other pointer is hovered on the element. Screen readers
  may announce the text as well.

I18n (Internationalization)

These two attributes allow you to specify the language and direction of
text in your document.

- `dir="ltr|rtl"`: This specifies the base directionality of the element's
  text content and tables. Typically, you don't need to set it anywhere
  on your page since the default is `ltr` (left-to-right). However, if your
  content's base directionality is right-to-left, such as in Hebrew, set
  `<html . . . dir="rtl" lang="he">` (sans ellipses) so the rest of the
  page inherits the setting. (Note: You should specify `lang`, too, as
  shown, but user agents don't determine text directionality from that).
  If you are intermingling left-to-right and right-to-left content, such as
  English and Arabic, respectively, set `dir` and `lang` on the element (a
  paragraph, for instance) that contains the content that deviates from
  the directionality of the page at large. Please also see the `bdo` element
  in Chapter 5 for a related discussion.

- `lang="`*language code*`"`: This specifies the language of the element's
  content. Be sure to always set it on the `html` element; elements on

the rest of the page inherit that value unless you override it at a more granular level. For instance, set <html . . . lang="en"> (sans ellipses) on a document in English. If a paragraph within that same page is in French, set <p lang="fr"> . . . </p> to override it. Please see the "Language Codes" section of this chapter to access more codes.

Events

These common event attributes allow you to assign JavaScript to a range of page behaviors. As a best practice, don't apply these attributes to your HTML inline as you do with other attributes. Meaning, avoid this: <a href="some-page.html" onclick="someFunction(); return false">link text</a>. Instead, use JavaScript to apply them unobtrusively; this is in keeping with the separation of content and behavior best practice described in "A Few Best Practices" earlier in this chapter. Search online for *unobtrusive JavaScript* to learn more and see code examples.

- **onclick="*script*"**: Event fires when the user clicks a mouse button or hits Return or Enter on the keyboard. (*Mouse* means *pointing device* for each event in this list.)

- **ondblclick="*script*"**: Event fires when the user double-clicks a mouse button.

- **onmousedown="*script*"**: Event fires when the user holds the mouse button down. This is the opposite of onmouseup.

- **onmouseup="*script*"**: Event fires when the user releases the mouse button. This is the opposite of onmousedown.

- **onmouseover="*script*"**: Event fires when the user moves the mouse cursor on top of an element. This is the opposite of onmouseout.

- **onmousemove="*script*"**: Event fires when the user moves the mouse cursor.

- **onmouseout="*script*"**: Event fires when the user moves the mouse cursor away from an item. This is the opposite of onmouseover.

- **onkeypress="*script*"**: Event fires when the user presses and releases a key.

- **onkeydown="*script*"**: Event fires when the user presses down on a key. This is the opposite of onkeyup.

- **onkeyup="*script*"**: Event fires when the user releases a key. This is the opposite of onkeydown.

Global (HTML5)

As discussed in the "How Attributes Are Noted in This Book" box, the attributes that HTML5 classifies as Global include X/HTML's Core, I18n, and Events, *plus* the unique ones listed here. The Global attributes may be applied to nearly every element in HTML5.

- **accesskey="*keyboard character*"**: (Note: Some X/HTML elements support tabindex, as noted in their entries in Part 2 of the book.) This attribute assigns a character as a shortcut to setting focus on an element, as in <input type="text" name="search" accesskey="4" />. Browsers and platforms vary on what key or keys you must press in combination with the accesskey to activate it. While pressing Ctrl plus the accesskey on a Mac typically activates the shortcut, on a Windows computer it's Alt for Internet Explorer and Chrome, Shift+Alt for Firefox, and Shift+Esc for Opera. Behavior varies per element and browser. See *http://www.webaim.org/techniques/keyboard/accesskey.php* for more information, including reasons why it hasn't gained wider adoption.

- **class**: Please see the description in the "Core" section.

- **contenteditable="true|false"**: HTML5 allows users to edit an element's content if the element has contenteditable="true". If contenteditable is not set, an element inherits the value from its nearest parent. A setting of `false` prevents an element from being edited. The default state is to inherit. For more information, see *http://blog.whatwg.org/the-road-to-html-5-contenteditable* and a demo at *http://html5demos.com/contenteditable*.

- **contextmenu="*id of* menu"**: This assigns the element's context menu when its value matches the `id` of a `menu` element (please see Chapter 15).

- **dir**: Please see the description in the "I18n" section.

- **draggable="true|false"**: HTML5 provides a drag and drop API. Set `draggable="true"` on an element to make it draggable (`false` does the opposite). If `draggable` is undefined, the default state is *auto*, which defers to the default state of the user agent.

- **hidden**: When present, this Boolean attribute "indicates that the element is not yet, or is no longer, relevant," and user agents shouldn't show the content. It affects presentation only; scripts and `form` controls in hidden content still work.

- **id**: Please see the description in the "Core" section.

- **itemid, itemprop, itemref, itemscope, and itemtype**: These attributes are related to defining microdata. Please see *http://dev.w3.org/html5/md/*.

- **lang**: Please see the description in the "I18n" section.

- **spellcheck="true|false"**: Set `spellcheck="true"` on an element whose content should have its spelling and grammar checked (`false` does the opposite). HTML5 suggests the default state could be for the element to inherit the setting of its parent but doesn't define it outright. It also doesn't define how a user agent should perform spell- and grammar-checking.

- **style**: Please see the description in the "Core" section.

- **tabindex="*number*"**: (Note: Some X/HTML elements support tabindex, as noted in their entries in Part 2 of the book.) Some users prefer to navigate a page with the Tab key (and Shift+Tab to move backward). Each time you press Tab in a supporting browser, the focus shifts to the next *a* element (a hyperlink or anchor) or form control according to the order in which it appears *in the HTML source*, not necessarily the on-screen order (because of CSS moving it).

  You may change the order by assigning a tabindex to an element, such as <a href="trees.html" tabindex="5">Trees</a>. Elements with tabindex gain priority, so they are tabbed to first (1 is the highest priority) before any other elements, regardless of source order. The numbers may be in any order or increment you'd like. The HTML source order determines the priority of elements with the same number. tabindex="0" has special meaning; it makes an element focusable by keyboard but places it in the normal document tabbing sequence. Also, tabindex on a disabled element has no effect since it can't gain focus.

  In HTML5, any negative number means you can't tab to the element, but you can set focus to it with JavaScript via focus(). Many browsers apply this same behavior to X/HTML documents when tabindex="-1".

  I strongly recommend you avoid using tabindex in most cases and make your natural tabbing order logical for users.

- **title**: Please see the description in the "Core" section.

Data Attributes

Data attributes are another of HTML5's particularly useful additions—they're custom attributes that you may apply to any element to store data in your HTML. They are helpful in cases where another attribute or element isn't appropriate for containing the information. You may name your attributes as you wish as long as they begin with data-. A data attribute's value doesn't appear in the page; instead, you leverage it with JavaScript. For example, imagine your page includes a list of products for males and females of all ages. By including data attributes, you could write a script that sorts or filters the list based on the user's choices.

Example:

```
<li data-gender="female" data-agerange="55-67">Product Name</
➥li>
```

You may add as many data attributes as necessary. For instance, the example could include another one called data-pricerange. Best of all, you can use data attributes today across browsers as long as your page has an HTML5 DOCTYPE. Please see *http://www.htmlfiver.com/data-attri-butes/* for an example of how to access your custom data with JavaScript.

Events That Are Part of Global

The HTML5 Global attribute set includes the X/HTML Events attributes. They are onclick, ondblclick, onkeydown, onkeypress, onkeyup, onmousedown, onmousemove, onmouseout, onmouseover, and onmouseup. Please see the "Events" section in this chapter for details. HTML5 also includes the following event-related attributes as part of Global:

onabort, onblur*, oncanplay, oncanplaythrough, onchange, oncontextmenu, ondrag, ondragend, ondragenter, ondragleave, ondragover, ondragstart, ondrop, ondurationchange, onemptied, onended, onerror*, onfocus*, onformchange, onforminput, oninput, oninvalid, onload*, onloadeddata, onloadedmetadata, onloadstart, onmousewheel, onpause, onplay, onplaying, onprogress, onratechange, onreadystatechange, onscroll, onseeked, onseeking, onselect, onshow, onstalled, onsubmit, onsuspend, ontimeupdate, onvolumechange, and onwaiting

Those with an asterisk have a different meaning when applied to the body element.

Please see the input element in Chapter 7 for details about onblur and onfocus. Descriptions for the others have been left out for space considerations and because many go beyond the scope of this book (for instance, many relate to scripting the audio and video elements). You can learn more at *http://www.w3.org/TR/html5/dom.html#global-attributes*.

Basic Data Types

This section describes basic HTML data types referenced by elements in Parts 2 and 3. Please also see *http://www.w3.org/TR/html4/types.html*.

CDATA, and id and name Attribute Values

The descriptions of many attributes indicate that CDATA is the accepted value, as in name="***cdata***" for form inputs. *CDATA*, in these instances, is a fancy name for a text string that accepts a variety of characters. Specifically, for id, name, and other attributes that accept text, their value "must begin with a letter ([A–Za–z]) and may be followed by any number of letters, digits ([0-9]), hyphens ('-'), underscores ('_'), colons (':'), and periods ('.')."

Character Encoding

The charset attribute defines the character encoding, such as what you should define in the head element of each document (see "Basic HTML Document Structure" earlier in this chapter and the meta element entry in Chapter 3). Most commonly, charset is set to utf-8. The W3C provides a thorough discussion on the topic at *http://www.w3.org/International/tutorials/tutorial-char-enc/*.

Content Types (MIME Types)

A *content type* specifies the nature of a linked or embedded resource, such as assigned to the type attribute of the link element that loads a style sheet. Among the common content types are `image/gif`, `image/png`, `image/svg+xml`, `text/css`, `text/javascript`, `text/html`, and `video/mpeg`. A complete list of registered MIME types is available at *http://www. w3.org/TR/html4/references.html#ref-MIMETYPES*.

Language Codes

A language code is assigned to the `lang` attribute to describe the language of an element's content, as in `lang="dl"` for Dutch. Please see the "l18n" section of this chapter for more details about `lang`. Language codes may have a subcode, too, as in `cn-zh`. Please see *http://www. anglistikguide.de/info/tools/languagecode.html* for a list of codes.

Link Types

The defined X/HTML link types are `alternate`, `stylesheet`, `start*`, `next`, `prev`, `contents*`, `glossary*`, `copyright*`, `chapter*`, `section*`, `subsection*`, `appendix*`, `help`, and `bookmark`. Please see *http://www.w3.org/TR/html4/types.html#h-6.12* for descriptions.

HTML5 includes the ones *not* marked with an asterisk and also includes these: `archives`, `author`, `external`, `icon`, `license`, `nofollow`, `noreferrer`, `pingback`, `prefetch`, `search`, `sidebar`, `tag`, `index`, `up`, `first`, and `last`. Please see *http://www.w3.org/TR/html5/interactive-elements.html# linkTypes* for descriptions. Additionally, HTML5 allows you to define new link types by defining them at *http://wiki.whatwg.org/wiki/RelExtensions*.

The `a` (Chapter 5), `link` (Chapter 3), and `area` (Chapter 6) elements use link types.

Character Entities

A character entity represents a character in a document's character set. Some common character entities are `&amp;` for an ampersand, ` ` for a nonbreaking space, < for a less-than sign, > for a greater-than sign, " for a straight quotation mark, ‘ for a curly opening single quotation mark, ’ for a curly closing single quotation mark, “ for a curly opening double quotation mark, and ” for a curly closing double quotation mark. There are dozens more. Here's a list, courtesy of Elizabeth Castro: *http://www.elizabethcastro.com/html/extras/entities.html*.

Deprecated and Obsolete Elements and Attributes

A *deprecated* element or attribute is one that you shouldn't use but that browsers still support for backward-compatibility reasons. Most of the deprecated items are presentational in nature and have been replaced by CSS. An *obsolete* element or attribute is one that you should not use and that browsers should not support.

The deprecated elements in X/HTML are applet, basefont, center, dir, font, isindex, menu, s, strike, and u.

The goal of this book is to be a practical reference to standards-based coding today and into the future. To that end, I deliberately left out obsolete and deprecated elements and obsolete attributes, since you shouldn't use them anyway. Similarly, I omitted proprietary (that is, nonstandard) elements that certain browsers support but that aren't part of any HTML specification, either final or in the works.

However, throughout Parts 2 (especially) and Part 3, I *do* note deprecated attributes and what you should use instead, which usually means using CSS to replace a presentational attribute. I also note elements and attributes that are valid in X/HTML but not in HTML5 (they're obsolete).

Part 2

HTML Elements and Guidance

This part of the book covers all nondeprecated elements that are shared among HTML 4, XHTML 1, and HTML5 (though some are obsolete in HTML5, as noted). Elements unique to HTML5 are covered in Part 3.

In some cases, an already existing element is different in HTML5, whether it's the element's meaning, the availability of an attribute, or the addition of new attributes. I note these differences throughout. In particular, keep an eye on the "Attributes in Detail" sections and the HTML5 boxes at the end of relevant entries. Each box details different uses and/or attributes for the element, allowing you to understand their application in HTML5 at a glance.

Part 2 Contents

2

Primary Structure and Sections

The elements in this chapter represent an HTML document's high-level structural and outline components. Some are essential (after all, you can't write an HTML document without the html element), while others are either used sparingly (the hr element) or have seen their usage decline in HTML5 (the div element).

This chapter is a counterpart to Chapter 11, which describes related elements unique to HTML5. If you're writing X/HTML documents, then you don't need to hop on over there. But, if you're writing HTML5, then this chapter and Chapter 11 combine to detail all the primary structural and sectioning elements at your disposal.

address

Author contact information

Syntax `<address></address>`

Attributes Core, I18n, Events, *HTML5 Only:* Global

Description

address is one of the most misleading elements by name. You'd logically think it's for marking up a postal address, but it isn't (except for one circumstance described in a little bit). In fact, surprisingly, there isn't an HTML element explicitly designed for that.

Instead, *address* defines contact information for the author of an HTML document or part of a document. It typically goes at either the beginning or, more often, the end of a page. However, if a section of a page has an author, place the *address* in context of that section.

Most of the time, contact information takes the form of the author's e-mail address or a link to a page with more contact information.

Example:

```
<address>
Page maintained by <a href="mailto:taylor.rose@yourdomain.com">
➥Taylor Rose</a> and <a href="/contact-us/katherine-whitney.
➥html">Katherine Whitney</a>.
</address>
```

Browsers typically render *address* content in italics by default, like this:

Page maintained by <u>Taylor Rose</u> and <u>Katherine Whitney</u>.

Additionally, the contact information could very well be the document author's postal address, in which case marking it up with address *would* be valid. But, if you're creating the Contact Us page for your business and want to include your office locations, it would be incorrect to code those with address. So, it's the context that matters.

HTML5 and the address Element

In HTML5, address pertains to the nearest article element ancestor, or the body if no article is present. It's customary to place address in an HTML5 footer element when documenting author contact information for the page at large.

An address in an article provides contact information for the author of that article within a document. Please see the article entry in Chapter 11 for an example.

HTML5 stipulates that address may contain author contact information only, not anything else such as the document or article's last modified date. Additionally, HTML5 forbids nesting any of the following elements inside address: h1–h6, address, article, aside, footer, header, hgroup, nav, and section.

body

Document content container

Syntax `<body>`
       `. . . [document content] . . .`
       `</body>`

Attributes Core, I18n, Events, `onload`, `onunload`, *HTML5 Only:* Global, `onafterprint`, `onbeforeprint`, `onbeforeunload`, `onblur`, `onerror`, `onfocus`, `onhashchange`, `onmessage`, `onoffline`, `ononline`, `onpagehide`, `onpageshow`, `onpopstate`, `onredo`, `onresize`, `onstorage`, `onundo`

Description

The body element contains all code related to a page's content and may also contain one or more `script` blocks. body is required for every HTML document except one that defines framesets, in which case it can appear only inside the `noframes` element. (Please see Chapter 10.) Only one body is allowed per HTML document.

Example:

```
. . .
</head>
<body>
    <h1>All about <code>body</code></h1>
    <p>The <code>body</code> element contains your page's
    content, which may include <em>nearly</em> every
    element.</p>
    . . .
</body>
</html>
```

body may contain text, images, objects, scripts, tables, and forms—in short, nearly every HTML element, whether block-level or inline. However, if the DOCTYPE is Strict (which I recommend), each inline element must be contained in a block-level element. For instance, the code and em elements in the example could not sit directly inside body because both are inline elements.

Attributes in Detail

In addition to the common events, body has two special event attributes (see the "HTML5 and the body Element" box, too):

- onload="*script*": Fires when all the document's content has finished loading. This includes all images, objects, and scripts (whether they are local to the site or external, third-party scripts). Consequently, the time it takes for onload to fire can vary greatly from page to page depending on the content, how content is served, network latency, a user's browser cache settings, and more.

- onunload="*script*": Fires when the user leaves the document, such as when navigating to another page via a link.

Deprecated Attributes

The following attributes are all presentational in nature, so use CSS instead to achieve the equivalent effect.

- alink: *Obsolete in HTML5.* This color appears as the user is selecting a link. Use the CSS a:active pseudo-selector to define the active link color instead.

- background: *Obsolete in HTML5.* Use the CSS background-image property to define the body background image instead.

- bgcolor: *Obsolete in HTML5.* Use the CSS background-color property to define the body background color instead.

- **link**: *Obsolete in HTML5*. Use the CSS `a:link` pseudo-selector to define the unvisited (that is, default) link color instead.

- **text**: *Obsolete in HTML5*. Use the CSS `color` attribute to define the default text color instead.

- **vlink**: *Obsolete in HTML5*. Use the CSS `a:visited` pseudo-selector to define the visited link color instead.

HTML5 and the body Element

HTML5 introduces several new event attributes to body. As with other events, it's best to apply these unobtrusively with JavaScript rather than include them in your HTML.

ATTRIBUTES IN DETAIL

- **onafterprint="*script*"**: This fires when the browser finishes printing the document.

- **onbeforeprint="*script*"**: This fires when the browser's Print functionality is engaged, such as when you choose Print from the menu but before the document has printed.

- **onbeforeunload="*script*"**: This fires just before the document unloads, which happens each time a user submits a form or navigates away from the current page. Use it if you want users to confirm they intend to leave the page.

- **onblur="*script*"**: This fires when body loses focus, such as when the user clicks the mouse pointer outside body. It's the opposite of onfocus.

- **onerror="*script*"**: This fires when an uncaught runtime script error occurs.

- **onfocus="*script*"**: This fires when the body achieves focus after having lost it. It's the opposite of onblur.

HTML5 and the body Element (continued)

- **onhashchange="*script*"**: This fires when only the hash (#) portion of the URL changes. For instance, if you are currently browsing *http://www.yourdomain.com/meteor-showers.html* and select a link that anchors to the #photos id elsewhere on the page, the URL changes to *http://www.yourdomain.com/meteor-showers.html#photos* and onhashchange fires if it's defined. It fires again if you navigate to another anchor or back to the initial state that had no hash.

- **onmessage="*script*"**: This fires when a document receives a message via server-sent events, Web sockets, cross-document messaging, and channel messaging. For example, HTML5's Cross-Document Messaging allows two documents to communicate regardless of their source domains. onmessage fires when one document receives a message from the other one via postMessage(). A full discussion of messaging is beyond the scope of this book.

- **onoffline="*script*"**: This fires when the navigator.onLine attribute value changes from true to false, which occurs when the browser cannot contact the network upon a user-initiated or programmatic request for a remote page or file.

- **ononline="*script*"**: The opposite of onoffline, this fires when the value of navigator.onLine changes from false to true.

- **onpagehide="*script*"**: This fires when navigating from a browser's *session history entry*, which is an individual URL and/or state object plus other contextual information. Loosely put, the *session history* represents the full set of pages accessed during a browsing session.

- **onpageshow="*script*"**: The opposite of onpagehide, this fires when navigating to a browser's session history entry.

(continues on next page)

HTML5 and the body Element (continued)

- **onpopstate="*script*"**: HTML5 allows you to manipulate the session history by recording an interface state (a *state object*) in the history programmatically. onpopstate fires when navigating to a browser's session history entry that is a state object. Please see *https://developer.mozilla.org/en/DOM/window.onpopstate* and *https://developer.mozilla.org/en/DOM/Manipulating_the_browser_history* for more information and examples.

- **onredo="*script*"**: HTML5's undo/redo history functionality is just one of its features that makes it easier to build robust Web applications. The concept is similar to the undo and redo features in word processors and other software. onredo fires when a redo operation takes place on an undo object. The specifics are beyond the scope of this book.

- **onresize="*script*"**: This fires when the body changes size.

- **onstorage="*script*"**: The W3C's Web Storage API (*http://www. w3.org/TR/webstorage/*), also referred to as "DOM Storage," allows you to store a large amount of data securely in the browser. onstorage fires when a storage event occurs. The specifics of Web Storage are beyond the scope of this book. Please see *http://dev. opera.com/articles/view/web-storage/* for more information.

- **onundo="*script*"**: This is the opposite of onredo, firing when an undo operation takes place on an undo object.

Also, when common events onblur, onerror, onfocus, and onload appear on body, they expose the same-named event handlers of the Window object. Please see "Attributes" in Chapter 1 for more details about these four events.

div

A generic container

Syntax

Attributes Core, I18n, Events, *HTML5 Only:* Global

Description

The div element serves as a generic, block-level container and has no semantic meaning. As is the case with any meaningless element, use div only when a proper semantic choice doesn't exist.

Developers typically use it in X/HTML as the wrapper around most primary blocks of content and then control the width, placement, and other presentation characteristics with CSS. div may contain both block-level and inline elements, including other divs.

Example:

```
<body>
<div id="container">
   <div id="header"> . . . </div>
   <div id="content">
      <div id="main"> . . . </div>
      <div id="sidebar"> . . . </div>
   </div>
   <div id="footer"> . . . </div>
</div>
</body>
```

 div's cousin is the span element, which is a generic, inline container with no semantic meaning.

Deprecated Attributes

- **align**: *Obsolete in HTML5.* align is presentational in nature, so instead use the CSS text-align property (with a value of center, justify, left, or right) to align a div's content.

HTML5 and the div Element

You'll find fewer instances to use div in HTML5 because that version of the language contains several containers that *do* have meaning, such as article, aside, header, footer, nav, and section (see Chapter 11). Use div only when a semantic element isn't required.

---

h1, h2, h3, h4, h5, h6

A heading

Syntax <h1></h1>
<h2></h2>
<h3></h3>
<h4></h4>
<h5></h5>
<h6></h6>

Attributes Core, I18n, Events, *HTML5 Only:* Global

Description

The h1–h6 elements represent content headings of varying degrees of importance. The h1 is the most important, and the h6 is the least. Each heading describes the content or functionality that follows, whether it's an article, a sign-up form, a module with a group of links, the title above an embedded video, and so on.

Your h1–h6 headings are among the most important elements in any HTML document, because they are integral to defining your page's outline. Plan them without regard for how you want them to look; focus on what heading hierarchy is appropriate for your content. This benefits both SEO and accessibility.

Search engines weigh your headings heavily, particularly the likes of h1. Screen reader users often navigate a page by headings, too, because it allows them to quickly assess a page's content without having to listen through every piece of content.

Opinions vary concerning whether it's appropriate to skip a heading level in a document—to move from h1 to h3 within a particular content area, for instance. Most people in the community think you should not skip a level, a view I share. Having said that, there is no firm rule in either X/HTML or HTML5 about this.

By default, headings typically render at a size comparable to its importance and in bold. However, as previously noted, don't use a particular heading level just because you want it to look a certain way. You can control all of that with CSS.

Example:

```
<h1>This is a heading level one</h1>
<h2>This is a heading level two</h2>
<h3>This is a heading level three</h3>
<h4>This is a heading level four</h4>
<h5>This is a heading level five</h5>
<h6>This is a heading level six</h6>
```

Please note that the following rendering isn't to scale.

This is a heading level one
This is a heading level two
This is a heading level three
This is a heading level four
This is a heading level five
This is a heading level six

Deprecated Attributes

- **align**: *Obsolete in HTML5.* align is presentational in nature, so instead use the CSS text-align property (with a value of center, justify, left, or right) to align a heading's content.

> **tip** You are allowed to use more than h1 per page, though it isn't common to do so and is mostly discouraged in X/HTML because the use cases are limited. Google's Matt Cutts has gone on record saying Google allows it without a search ranking penalty as long as it's content-appropriate and within reason. However, you *should* use h1 more often in an HTML5 document. See the "HTML5 and the h1–h6 Elements" box.

> **tip** You'll often see the h1 used to wrap a site's logo, but I don't recommend this practice in X/HTML. Save your h1 for the main heading (or two) within your content.

HTML5 and the h1–h6 Elements

HTML5's article, aside, nav, section, and hgroup elements greatly impact the way in which you use h1–h6 headings. Please see the "HTML5's Document Outline" section and the elements' entries in Chapter 11.

---

hr

A horizontal rule

Syntax <hr> or <hr />

Attributes Core, I18n, Events, *HTML5 Only:* Global

Description

The hr element does not contain any content; it renders as a horizontal rule, acting as a separator.

Example:

```
<p>This is a paragraph.</p>
<hr />
<p>This is another paragraph.</p>
```

By default, user agents typically render it as a two-color (gray), 2-pixel-high bar that extends the full width of the content container in which it sits. The space above and below an hr tends to vary among browsers.

This is a paragraph.

This is another paragraph.

Deprecated Attributes

- **align**: *Obsolete in HTML5.* Use the CSS width and, optionally, margin properties to dictate the alignment of an hr relative to the content around it.

- **noshade**: *Obsolete in HTML5.* This Boolean attribute, when present, turns off the default "groove" appearance of an hr by rendering the

two lines in one color instead of two. Use CSS instead, such as
hr { border: 1px solid #999; }, where #999 represents the color.

- **size**: *Obsolete in HTML5*. Use the CSS height property to dictate the
  size instead.

- **width**: *Obsolete in HTML5*. Use the CSS width property to dictate the
  width instead.

HTML5 and the hr Element

HTML5 gives the hr more context by redefining it as "a paragraph-
level thematic break, e.g. a scene change in a story, or a transition to
another topic within a section of a reference book."

---

html

Document root element

Syntax <html></html>

Attributes I18n, *HTML5 Only:* Global, manifest

Description

The html element is the root element of every HTML document; all
other elements are contained within it. The opening html tag should be
preceded by a valid DOCTYPE.

Example (typical HTML 4 Strict document):

```
<!DOCTYPE HTML PUBLIC "-//W3C//DTD HTML 4.01//EN"
"http://www.w3.org/TR/html4/strict.dtd">
```

```
<html lang="en">
<head>
   . . .
</head>
<body>
   . . .
</body>
</html>
```

The lang attribute sets the base language for the entire document. The structure remains the same as the example for other versions of HTML, except for the DOCTYPE and, in some cases, the attributes on html. Please see Chapter 1 for more information about lang, the html element's other attributes, and DOCTYPE options.

Deprecated Attributes

- **version:** *Obsolete in HTML5.* Do not use this attribute since it provides redundant information as the DOCTYPE regarding the required DTD version.

HTML5 and the html Element

If the previous example had been an HTML5 document, everything would be the same except the DOCTYPE would be <!DOCTYPE html>.

ATTRIBUTES IN DETAIL

- **manifest="*URL*":** This optional attribute contains a valid non-empty URL that points to the document's application cache manifest. HTML5 provides the means to run offline Web applications

(continues on next page)

HTML5 and the `html` Element (continued)

(*application* can mean a robust application or just a handful of HTML pages; it doesn't matter). The *application cache manifest* lists the files an application needs to operate when disconnected from the network. The browser saves a copy of the files when you access the site online. Details about offline Web applications are beyond the scope of this book, but you specify the attribute like this:

```
<html manifest="myapplication.manifest">
```

Please note that a `base` element has no effect on resolving a relative URL in the `manifest` attribute since `manifest` is processed before `base` appears.

3

Document Head

An HTML document's head element contains important information about the page, links to external resources such as style sheets, and embedded styles, when necessary. Plus, what you include in your page's head impacts search engine optimization (SEO).

Each of the elements described in this chapter may appear only in the head, except style, which has an exception in HTML5.

note The script element may also appear in the head; however, it's best to include it at the end of your page just before the </body> end tag whenever possible.

base

Document's base URI

Syntax `<head>`
       `<base href="">` or `<base href="" />`
    `</head>`

Attributes href, target, *HTML5 Only:* Global

Description

The base element defines the page's absolute URI from which relative paths to external resources are resolved. (External resources include assets such as images, JavaScript files, and style sheets, as well as links to other pages and paths to server-side scripts that process forms.) base must be defined in the document head before any element that calls upon an external resource, and there can be only one base element per page. If base is not defined, the page's base URI defaults to the current page. Most pages on the Web don't define base because the default behavior is what is desired.

Attributes in Detail

- **href="*uri*"**: Defines the document's base absolute URI.

- **target**: Used to set the base target for links and form actions in documents with frame or iframe elements. Please see the frame entry in Chapter 10 for more information.

It's important to note that base impacts the URIs only for the page in which it appears. For instance, if you define background-image: url(../img/arrow.png) in an external style sheet that is loaded by a page with base defined, the path to the image is unaffected. Similarly, base in a parent document does not affect the paths within an iframe's document. Lastly, the object element's codebase attribute takes precedence over base.

The easiest way to understand how base works is to see examples both with and without it. Let's say you've created the following page at *http://www.myvacationpics.com/2009/*.

Example 1 (without base defined):

```
<head>
   . . .
   <link rel="stylesheet" href="../css/global.css"
   type="text/css" />
</head>
<body>
   . . .
   <p>
      <img src="image/kauai/thumbnail_volcano_01.jpg"
      width="400" height="300" alt="Kauai volcano" />
      <a href="volcanoes/kauai.html">Kauai Volcano Pics</a>
   </p>
   . . .
</body>
```

Example 1 is your typical HTML page—the paths to the external assets are exactly how they appear in the code. That is, the paths to the style sheet, the volcano image, and the page to view more pictures are relative to the HTML page's location, which is in the /2009/ directory.

Now, let's apply a base value while leaving the rest of the code exactly as it was in Example 1. Remember, you aren't moving the page to a different folder, just adding base to the page.

Example 2 (with base defined):

```
<head>
   . . .
   <base href="http://www.myvacationpics.com/2010/" />
   <link rel="stylesheet" href="../css/global.css"
   type="text/css" />
</head>
<body>
   . . .
   <p>
      <img src="image/kauai/thumbnail_volcano_01.jpg"
      width="400" height="300" alt="Kauai volcano" />
      <a href="volcanoes/kauai.html">Kauai Volcano Pics</a>
   </p>
   . . .
</body>
```

With the base defined in Example 2, all URIs in the page are now relative to the base href value, meaning the page treats them as if it's in the /2010/ directory even though it still lives in /2009/. Here are the paths as they appear in the code and where the page looks for them now that they resolve to new locations:

- ../css/global.css resolves to *http://www.myvacationpics.com/css/global.css* (this didn't change because of the path).

- image/kauai/thumbnail_volcano_01.jpg now resolves to *http://www.myvacationpics.com/2010/image/kauai/thumbnail_volcano_01.jpg* (instead of *http://www.myvacationpics.com/2009/image/kauai/thumbnail_volcano_01.jpg*, as in Example 1).

- volcanoes/kauai.html resolves to *http://www.myvacationpics.com/2010/volcanoes/kauai.html* (instead of *http://www.myvacationpics.com/2009/volcanoes/kauai.html*, as in Example 1).

head

Information about document

Syntax <head>

    . . .

    </head>

Attributes I18n, profile*, *HTML5 Only:* Global

Description

The head element is required in each HTML document. It houses a handful of other elements that provide information about the page, such as the character encoding, title, links to style sheets, and metadata for search engines. It does not contain page content (as the body element does) that user agents generally render, though they may surface the information in other ways (such as with title on the title bar).

The elements that head may contain are base, link, meta, script, style, and title. All are defined in this chapter except script, which is covered in Chapter 9. Also, all of these except script (and style in HTML5) may appear only in the head.

The head immediately follows the DOCTYPE and the html element, as shown in the example.

Example:

```
<!DOCTYPE html PUBLIC "-//W3C//DTD XHTML 1.0 Strict//EN"
"http://www.w3.org/TR/xhtml1/DTD/xhtml1-strict.dtd">
<html xmlns="http://www.w3.org/1999/xhtml" xml:lang="en"
lang="en">
<head>
```

(continues on next page)

```
    <title>Sunny renewable green energy services - Solar
    Panels Galore</title>
    <meta http-equiv="Content-Type" content="text/html;
    charset=utf-8" />
    . . . [other meta elements] . . .
    <link rel="stylesheet" type="text/css"
    href="/common/css/base.css" />
</head>
<body>
. . .
```

Attributes in Detail

- **profile="*uri*"**: *Obsolete in HTML5*. As I mention in this chapter's entry
  for the meta element, you may create your own meta elements simply
  by including them in your page. You may also create a metadata
  profile, which is documentation of a metadata standard, and point to
  it with the profile attribute on the head. It's a way of informing user
  agents that some of your meta elements are derived from that profile.
  Including the profile attribute does not change the behavior of the
  meta elements, however. A full discussion of profiles is beyond the
  scope of this book, but you can read more at *http://www.w3.org/TR/
  html401/struct/global.html#profiles*. Also, two such profiles are Dublin
  Core (*http://dublincore.org/documents/dces/* and *http://dublincore.org/
  resources/faq/*) and XFN (*http://gmpg.org/xfn/11* and *http://micro
  formats.org/wiki/xfn*).

HTML5 and the head Element

HTML5 declares the profile attribute obsolete and in its place requests you register extensions to the predefined set of metadata names (application-name, author, description, and generator, as discussed in the meta entry in this chapter). You may register extensions at *http://wiki.whatwg.org/wiki/MetaExtensions*.

link

Link to a related resource

Syntax   <link rel="" href=""> or <link rel="" href="" />

Attributes   Core, I18n, Events, charset*, href, hreflang, media, rel, rev*, target*, type, *HTML5 Only:* Global, sizes

Description

The link element defines a link between the current document and another resource, but in a much different way than the a element. Like a, link uses the href attribute to define the location of the resource, but link doesn't display actionable text in your page content. Instead, it provides information for user agents to act upon. A page may have multiple link elements, and they must always appear in the head element.

There are two cases for using link:

■ To link to a resource that affects the current view, such as a style sheet or favicon. Please see Examples 1–4.

■ To link to a resource that doesn't affect the page but that is related to it, such as a version in an alternate format (RSS or Atom feed, PDF,

and so on) or language, or to link to a resource that is part of the same
series of documents, such as chapters split into multiple HTML files.
Again, these links are not displayed in your page content, but a search
engine may index the related documents, and in the case of a feed, an
RSS reader displays the linked XML content. Please see Examples 5–7.

The best way to get a feel for link is to look at some examples.

Linking to Style Sheets or a Favicon

The most common use for link by far is to load a style sheet.

Example 1 (load a style sheet):

```
<head>
    . . .
    <link rel="stylesheet" href="/common/css/base.css"
    type="text/css" media="screen, print" />
    . . .
</head>
```

> **tip** You may have seen style sheets loaded with @import, too. However,
> using link is a best practice, primarily because style sheets load as
> fast as or faster than @import in a range of scenarios.

It doesn't matter in what order the attributes appear, but the sequence
in Example 1 is pretty standard. Also, it's customary to include the type
attribute as shown whenever you load a style sheet, and rel will always
be either "stylesheet" or "alternate stylesheet" (see Example 3). The
href and media attributes will vary, however. href provides the URI (an
absolute path, in this case) to the style sheet, and media defines in what
media the style sheet should be applied to the page (screen layout and
when printing, in the example). Please see "Attributes in Detail" for more
options.

Now let's load two style sheets.

Example 2 (load two or more style sheets):

```
<link rel="stylesheet" href="/common/css/base.css"
type="text/css" media="screen" />
<link rel="stylesheet" href="/common/css/print.css"
type="text/css" media="print" />
```

Use two or more link elements if you have separate style sheets for displaying your page on-screen and printing (or other purposes as defined by media). This is pretty common, since there are often elements you want to "turn off" for printing, such as navigation and ads.

The final style sheet example shows how to load an alternate style sheet, which you use to provide a different presentation than your default layout. It could be for a different theme (light on dark versus dark on light), changing the dimensions, and so on.

Example 3 (load an alternate style sheet):

```
<link rel="stylesheet" href="/common/css/base.css"
type="text/css" media="screen" title="Default" />
<link rel="stylesheet" href="/common/css/print.css"
type="text/css" media="print" />
<link rel="alternate stylesheet" href="/common/css/theme-
➥light-on-dark.css" type="text/css" media="screen"
title="Light on Dark" />
```

Your page may have several alternate style sheets. An alternate style sheet doesn't affect your page by default. Some browsers allow you to select it from a menu as listed per its title attribute. For instance, in Firefox's View > Page Style menu, you'd see the Default and Light on Dark themes to choose from for Example 3. Since not all browsers provide a means to select an alternate style sheet, developers often implement a JavaScript style switcher (search online for more details).

Now it's time to move onto the second most frequent use of link: displaying a favicon.

Example 4 (display a favicon):

```
<link rel="shortcut icon" href="/img/favicon.ico"
type="image/x-icon" />
```

A *favicon* is the small site-specific icon you'll often see in a browser's address bar before the URL, next to a bookmark/favorite, on a tab (depending on the browser), or on a desktop shortcut (depending on the OS). If favicon.ico lives at your site root, you typically don't need to use link, though you may prefer to just be explicit. Note that if you use rel="icon" instead of rel="shortcut icon", Internet Explorer won't load it. (Even so, older versions of IE exhibit some inconsistent favicon behavior. You may need to bookmark the page before the favicon will show.)

Linking to Related Documents

The remaining examples demonstrate using link to point to related documents that don't impact the page's layout.

Example 5 (point to RSS or Atom feed):

```
<link rel="alternate" type="application/rss+xml" href=
➥ "topstories.xml" title="Top Stories -- YourDomain.com" />
```

The link format in Example 5 tells an RSS reader where to locate your feed. Note the values for the rel and type attributes. You may have more than one feed per document, such as one link for national top stories and another for regional news. For an Atom feed, specify type="application/atom+xml" instead.

Example 6 (point to alternate language):

```
<link rel="alternate" type="text/html" hreflang="es"
href="spanish.html" title="Article in Spanish" />
```

If you provide a link to an alternate language version of the document, as in Example 6, a search engine may index it. Note the use of the `hreflang` attribute. `type` is set to `text/html` to reflect that the `href` points to a document with that content type.

Example 7 (point to documents in a series, and prefetching)

```
<link rel="start" href="step-one.html" />
<link rel="prev" href="step-four.html" />
<link rel="next" href="step-six.html" />
```

Let's say you've written a series of pages called "The Seven Steps to Creating Your Own Luck." If `step-five.html` were the current document, it could include the `link` elements shown in Example 7, which inform search engines about the series. `rel="start"` refers to the first document in the series.

Furthermore, Firefox prefetches a `rel="next"` href. This means that in Example 7, the assets for `step-six.html` are loaded behind the scenes as you're browsing the current page. You don't have to prefetch an entire page, though. The href attribute could just as easily point to an image or a style sheet. The former would be handy if the current page is one of several within a photo gallery, for example.

> **note** Firefox 3.0+ also supports `rel="prefetch"`, which is the HTML5 way to specify a resource for prefetching (HTML5 supports next, too). Other browsers may follow suit.

> **tip** Learn more about prefetching at *https://developer.mozilla.org/en/ Link_prefetching_FAQ*.

Attributes in Detail

(See the "HTML5 and the link Element" box for additional details.)

- **charset**: **Obsolete in HTML5*. This specifies the character encoding of the link destination. Please see "Character Encoding" in Chapter 1 for more details.

- **href="*uri*"**: This defines the link resource location. Please see the *a* element in Chapter 5 for a description of various URI paths that are available to you.

- **hreflang="*langcode*"**: Not often used, this indicates the base language of the href's destination, much in the way the lang attribute specifies the language of other HTML elements. Hence, you may use hreflang only when href is present. See Example 6.

- **media**: When rel is set to stylesheet, this comma-separated list indicates the media for which the style sheet applies (see Examples 1–3). If you leave out media, the value typically defaults to all in browsers, even though HTML 4 declares it should be screen.

  The following list includes the possible media values. screen and print enjoy wide support and, with all, are used the most by a very large margin. Support for the others varies. Please also see the "HTML5 and the link Element" box.

  - **all**: For all devices.
  - **aural**: For speech synthesizers.
  - **braille**: For Braille assistive devices.
  - **handheld**: For handheld devices, but few support it. Typically, you'll use screen instead when designing for mobile.

- **print**: For printing and print preview.
- **projection**: For projectors and similar views. Opera's projection mode, Opera Show, supports it.
- **screen**: For typical computer screens and modern mobile browsers. This is the value that tells a Web browser to render a style sheet.
- **tty**: For media using a fixed-pitch character grid, such as teletypes.
- **tv**: For television-type devices.

- **rel="*link-types*"** and **rev="*link-types*"**: *rev is obsolete in HTML5.* rel and rev have opposite meanings and are used in conjunction with href. The rel attribute indicates the relationship from the current document to the linked resource (see Examples 1–7). rev ("reverse") indicates the relationship from the linked resource to the current document. (Please see the *a* element in Chapter 5 for a full description of the difference.)

- **target**: *Not valid with Strict HTML 4 and XHTML 1 DOCTYPEs. Obsolete in HTML5.* target specifies the name of the frame for which the link applies. HTML provides four special target names with specific behavior: _blank, _self, _parent, and _top. Please see Chapter 10 for more details.

- **type="*content-type*"**: Tells the user agent the content type of the content at the link's destination. It is only advisory.

HTML5 and the link Element

HTML5 requires link to have a rel attribute, an itemprop attribute, or both. Please see "Attributes" in Chapter 1 concerning itemprop, an HTML5 global attribute.

HTML5 also allows link inside a noscript element that's in the head.

ATTRIBUTES IN DETAIL

HTML5 expands the values for media and includes the sizes attribute.

- **media**: This attribute's list of values is the same as in X/HTML except that it includes media queries. In HTML5, media's value must be a valid media query list from the Media Queries specification (*http://www.w3.org/TR/2009/CR-css3-mediaqueries-2009 0915/#syntax*). media is allowed only if href is present.

- **sizes**: This defines the size(s) of a linked icon(s). sizes="all" means the icon is scalable, such as an SVG image. Otherwise, provide a space-delimited list of sizes (if more than one) in *WIDTHxHEIGHT* format, where each value is a non-negative integer.

Examples:

```
<link rel="icon" href="some-icon.svg" sizes="any"
type="image/svg+xml">
<link rel="icon" href="favicon.png" sizes="16x16"
type="image/png">
<link rel="icon" href="icon-set.icns" sizes="16x16 128x128
➥ 256x256">
```

meta

Document metadata

Syntax   <head>
    <meta> or <meta />
  </head>

Attributes   I18n, content, http-equiv, name, scheme*, *HTML5 Only:*
Global, charset

Description

View source on virtually any Web page, and you're bound to see a handful of meta elements—typically called meta *tags*—in the head element.
meta specifies information about the current HTML document in a name-
value pair format, primarily for the benefit of browsers, search engine
spiders, and other user agents. Metadata does not appear in your page's
content. There's no limit to the number of meta elements you can include
in your page as long as all of them are in the head.

Example 1 shows arguably the most important meta element.

Example 1 (declaring the content type):

```
<head>
    <title>. . .</title>
    <meta http-equiv="Content-Type" content="text/html;
    ➥ charset=utf-8" />
    . . .
</head>
```

The name in the name-value pair in this example is the http-equiv
attribute, while content, as always, is the value. Include this meta

element in each of your pages to define your document's character encoding (UTF-8, in this case). It's standard practice to make it one of the first elements inside the head, either just before or just after the title. (HTML5 changes the syntax for this usage of meta. Please see the charset attribute in the "HTML5 and the meta Element" box.)

> **tip** It's important to add a Content-Type meta element to your documents so user agents can detect the document's character encoding. If you exclude it, you run the risk of your users seeing unreadable text, particularly on a multilingual site. For more information, see *http://www.w3.org/International/ tutorials/tutorial-char-enc/*.

Typically, meta elements are grouped together, though they don't have to be. And there's no set list of meta element name-value properties from which to choose. You're allowed to create your own simply by including them in your page (or you can create them more formally; see the head element's profile attribute in this chapter). But, the following are among the most common ones, and they define information that search engines use to varying degrees.

Example 2 (common meta elements):

```
<head>
    <title>Sunny renewable green energy services - Solar
Panels Galore</title>
    <meta http-equiv="Content-Type" content="text/html;
    ➥ charset=utf-8" />
    <meta name="description" content="Solar Panels Galore
    provides consulting and installation services for
    industrial, commercial and residential active and
    passive solar panel systems." />                    (continues on next page)
```

```
<meta name="keywords" content="solar panels, active solar,
passive solar, renewable energy, green energy, solar
panel installation, solar panel consultation,
industrial, commercial, residential" />
<meta name="author" content="Tanya Brown" />

    . . .
</head>
```

The most useful of the three highlighted meta elements in Example 2 is
name="description". A search engine may display this value as a snip-
pet of text in its search results. So, I highly recommend you include a
succinct, informative description in each page. Search engines don't all
display the same number of characters, though, so limit yours to 150–160.

The impact of name="keywords" metadata (see Example 2) on search
engine ranking has diminished dramatically over the years, to the point
that Google declared that it completely ignores name="keywords" for
Web search. Some search engines still use them (though not heavily), so
continue to include them, as long as they are relevant to your content.
They fell out of favor because many unscrupulous site owners tried to
trick search engines by including popular keywords that were unrelated
to their site's content. Search engines got wise to this and put more
emphasis on a site's body content and far less on meta keywords.

The name="author" metadata is similar in that a search engine spider or
other user agent may choose to use it.

tip   Use the following meta element to tell a search engine to neither
index the page content nor follow any of the links on it. You may also
specify noindex or nofollow individually.

```
<meta name="robots" content="noindex, nofollow" />
```

tip Microsoft introduced the X-UA-Compatible header in IE8 to allow you to dictate the IE version your page should render as. For example, this tells it to behave like IE7's standards mode:

`<meta http-equiv="X-UA-Compatible" content="IE=7" />`

Of course, it's best to make your page work in the latest version of IE instead of forcing it to behave like IE7, but there may be times when this meta element is necessary. Learn more about the modes at *http://www.htmlfiver.com/extras/meta/*.

Attributes in Detail

- **content**: This is the "value" in the name-value pair of a meta element.

- **http-equiv**: Also called a *pragma directive*, this behaves like an HTTP header sent by the server. Along with the name attribute, http-equiv is one of the "names" in the name-value pair of a meta element. It must be paired with content. See Example 1.

- **name**: As you would expect, this represents a "name" in the name-value pair of a meta element. It must be paired with content.

- **scheme**: *Obsolete in HTML5*. You may populate scheme with text of your choosing that clarifies a meta's content. For instance, `<meta name="date" content="11-05-2010" scheme="DD-MM-YYYY" />` explains the date refers to May 11, not November 5.

HTML5 and the meta Element

Each meta element must include the charset, http-equiv, itemprop, or name attribute, but not more than one, and the content attribute is required in tandem with all but charset.

ATTRIBUTES IN DETAIL

- **charset:** Exclusive to HTML5 on meta, charset specifies the document's character encoding. You may define it only once in a page. The Content-Type meta syntax in Example 1 technically is still allowed in HTML5, but the preferred format is highlighted next, which I recommend you use. Furthermore, HTML5 requires it to appear within the first 512 bytes (that is, characters) of your code. You'll always be safe if you put it before the title.

```
<!DOCTYPE html>
<html lang="en">
<head>
     <meta charset="utf-8"/> <!-- use instead of Example
1 format -->
   <title>. . .</title>
   . . . [other meta elements] . . .
   . . .
</head>
. . .
```

- **name:** HTML5 defines a set of four metadata names, though you still may use others. The *http://wiki.whatwg.org/wiki/ MetaExtensions* page documents extensions to this predefined set, and you can register your own by adding them to the wiki.

  Two of the predefined names are author and description, which you use just as I showed in Example 2. The other two are as follows:

  – application-name: Defines a short Web application name, but use it only if your page represents a Web application; here's an

  (continues on next page)

HTML5 and the meta Element (continued)

example: `<meta name="application-name" content="Inventory Manager">`. This attribute may appear only once in a page.

- **generator**: Specifies the name of the tool, if any, used to generate the document; here's an example: `<meta name="generator" content="Dreamweaver">`. Do not include it if you hand-code a page.

- **http-equiv**: HTML5 formally defines four standard values:

  - **content-language**: HTML5 discourages you from using this and recommends the `lang` attribute on the `html` element instead.

  - **content-type**: This defines the document's content type, as shown in Example 1, but use the `charset` attribute instead for HTML5.

  - **default-style**: This sets the name of the default alternate style sheet.

  - **refresh**: This instructs a page to refresh after a specified period of time. Your page may include only one instance. A `meta` `refresh` takes one of two forms: a number of seconds or a number of seconds and a URL.

    For example, if your page were a sports scoreboard, you would direct it to refresh every 90 seconds with `<meta http-equiv="refresh" content="90">`.

    Include a URL if you want to refresh to a different page after the specified number of seconds. A use case for this is a photo gallery that autocycles every 10 seconds: `<meta http-equiv="refresh" content="10; url=photo-06.html">`. However, avoid using this if you've moved content from one location to another and want to redirect users coming into the old location via a search engine or bookmark. Use a 301 Redirect instead (please search online for more information.)

style

An embedded style sheet

Syntax
```
<head>
    <style type="text/css">
    . . .
    </style>
</head>
```

Attributes l18n, media, title, type, *HTML5 Only:* Global, scoped

Description

In most cases, it's best to put your CSS in an external style sheet and link to it, because it's easier to manage and takes advantage of caching to speed up your pages. The style element is for those occasions when you want to embed CSS in your page. Your page may include multiple style elements, but they may appear only in the head element, except in HTML5 (see the "HTML5 and the style Element" box).

If you were to define the same CSS selector in each of the three style sheets in the example that follows, the order in which they appear determines which definition is applied to the page. For instance, if the linked base.css in the example specifies p { font-size: 1em; color: #333; }, then the rule in the style block overwrites the font-size value. In turn, subpage.css overwrites any conflicting p { . . . } property values in both base.css and the style block because it's last. The exception is if the media attribute differs on any of the three. If the style block had media="print" instead, its rules would not impact base.css, and subpage.css would *only* impact base.css.

Example:

```
<head>
   . . .
   <link rel="stylesheet" href="base.css" type="text/css"
   media="screen" />

   <!-- overwrites conflicting rules in base.css -->
   <style type="text/css" media="screen">
   p {
      font-size: 1.2em;
   }
   . . .
   </style>

   <!-- overwrites conflicting rules in base.css and style
   element -->
   <link rel="stylesheet" href="subpage.css" type="text/css"
   media="screen" />
</head>
```

Attributes in Detail

(Please see the "HTML5 and the style Element" box for more attribute information.)

- **media**: This optional comma-separated list indicates the media for which the style sheet applies. If you leave out media, the value typically defaults to all in browsers, even though HTML 4 declares it should be screen. Please see the link element entry in this chapter for more details, including an explanation of possible media values.

- **title="*text*"**: The title attribute is supposed to be advisory in this context, but it does impact behavior in some browsers. Namely, if a title is specified, some versions of Chrome, Firefox, and Safari treat the style block like an alternate style sheet and *don't render the styles* unless the user selects the alternate style sheet. Only Firefox makes it easy to choose it (View > Page Style). See the "HTML5 and the style Element" box for more. So, use title only if you intend to implement a JavaScript style switcher (search online for more details).

- **type**: "*Required.*" This attribute with a value of text/css must appear on each style element.

 Please see the link element in this chapter regarding loading an external style sheet.

HTML5 and the style Element

HTML5 also allows style inside a noscript element in the head as well as most elements with the scoped attribute in the document's body.

ATTRIBUTES IN DETAIL

HTML5 has an additional attribute, scoped, and gives title special meaning on style.

- **scoped**: Unlike X/HTML, HTML5 allows one or more style elements in the body element as long as this Boolean attribute is present. And if it is present, it means the style element applies to its parent element and the parent's child nodes only. In the following example, only the second article element and its children receive the rules defined in the scoped style element. However, mixing CSS and HTML is not a good practice and presents maintenance headaches, so I recommend you use a scoped style element only if you have a special case that can't be solved by an external style sheet.

(continues on next page)

HTML5 and the style Element (continued)

Example:

```
<body>
   . . .
   <article><!-- this doesn't receive padding -->
     <h1>This is not affected</h1>
     <p>This is not affected.</p>
   </article>

   <article><!-- this receives padding -->
     <style type="text/css" scoped>
     article { padding: 25px; }
     h1 { color: blue; }
     p { color: red; }
     </style>

     <h1>This is blue.</h1>
     <p>This is red.</p>
   </article>
   . . .
</body>
```

■ **title**: If a title is present, it defines the style element as an alternate style sheet.

title

The document's title

Syntax
```
<head>
    <title></title>
</head>
```

Attributes I18n, *HTML5 Only:* Global

Description

The title element defines a document's title and may contain both plain text and character entities but not markup. It is required for each HTML document (except HTML5 emails) and must be defined within a document's head element, and only once. The title value displays at the top of the browser window rather than in the Web page.

The title text also serves as the bookmark title when you bookmark a page, unless you edit it manually. As a best practice, choose title text that briefly summarizes a document's content. This benefits both screen reader users and your search engine rankings (please see the "The title Element and SEO" box). Secondarily, indicate your site's name in the title.

I recommend you get your title's core message into the first 60 characters, including spaces, because search engines often cut them off in their results at around that number (as a baseline). Browsers display a varying number of characters, but more than 60, in the title bar before cutting off the text.

Example:
```
<head>
    <title>Photos of the Kauai Volcano | MyVacationPics.com
    ➥</title>
. . .
</head>
```

The title element should not be confused with the title attribute
(please see "Attributes" in Chapter 1).

The title Element and SEO

Many developers—even well-intentioned, fairly experienced ones—
often give little consideration to the title element. They'll simply
put the name of their site and then copy it across all HTML pages (or
even worse, leave the title text their code editor inserts by default).
However, if one of your goals is to drive traffic to your site, you'd be
doing yourself and your potential readers a huge disservice by following suit.

Search engines have different algorithms that determine a page's
rank and how its content is indexed; universally, though, title plays
a key role. First, most search engines look to the title element for
an indication of what a page is about and index a page's content in
search of related text. An effective title focuses on a handful of keywords that are central to a page's content.

Second, search engines use the title element as the linked title that
appears in their search results listings. If you're like me, and I suspect
the majority of users, you scan the titles in the list of search results
first when you're trying to determine which page seems to match
what you're seeking. The more targeted your title text, the more
likely it is to show up in the results and be chosen by a user.

SEO is a deep topic, and I highly encourage you to do more research
on your own. But, I hope this gives you both a glimpse into one of
SEO's key components and the incentive to craft strategic title elements, if you aren't doing so already.

4

Lists

HTML affords you three list types: definition list (dl), ordered list (ol), and unordered list (ul). I explain each in depth in their respective entries in this chapter.

Lists are one of the most commonly used semantic elements across the Web. This is particularly true of unordered lists, which are ubiquitous as the choice for marking up navigation and many other groups of links.

Before I explain each list-related element, I'll discuss a capability that is common to all lists: nesting.

Nested Lists

Lists can be nested within other lists, as shown in the following example that details a sequenced plan to relocate. In this case, it's an ordered list inside another one, though you can nest any type of list within any other type (see the dl entry in this chapter for a related note).

```
<ol>
    <li>Take an Italian Berlitz course.</li>
    <li>Move to Italy.
        <!-- Start nested list -->
        <ol>
            <li>Have a yard sale.</li>
            <li>Pack what's left.</li>
            <li>Ship boxes.</li>
            <li>Jump on plane.</li>
        </ol>
        <!-- end nested list -->
    </li><!-- close list item containing nested list -->
    <li>Say &ldquo;Ciao!&rdquo; upon landing.</li>
</ol>
```

This displays by default in most user agents as shown here:

1. Take an Italian Berlitz course.
2. Move to Italy.
    1. Have a yard sale.
    2. Pack what's left.
    3. Ship boxes.
    4. Jump on plane.
3. Say "Ciao!" upon landing.

There's one simple but important rule to follow when nesting lists: You must insert the nested list *inside* an li element (or dd element in the case of a definition list) of the parent list. That is, putting the list *alongside* a parent li or dd is invalid.

Also, although this example shows only one level of nesting, you can also nest a list inside a nested list (and another inside that one, *ad infinitum*). For example, I could nest an unordered list (a ul, as you'll recall) in the "Pack what's left" li to list all items to pack, irrespective of packing order.

dd

A definition description

Syntax <dd></dd>

Attributes Core, I18n, Events, *HTML5 Only*: Global

Description

Use the dd element to describe a corresponding term (dt) in a *definition list* (dl). The dd follows the dt and may contain block-level content, such as paragraphs (p), ordered lists (ol), unordered lists (ul), another definition list, and more.

 If your dd content is longer than one paragraph, nest ps in the dd rather than splitting the text among multiple dds without ps.

Example:

```
<h2>1936 Summer Olympics 100m Men's Results</h2>
<dl>
    <dt>Gold medal winner</dt>
    <dd>Jesse Owens (USA)</dd>

    <dt>Silver medal winner</dt>
    <dd>Ralph Metcalfe (USA)</dd>

    <dt>Bronze medal winner</dt>
    <dd>Tinus Osendarp (NED)</dd>
</dl>
```

The simplest arrangement within a dl is one dt grouped with one dd, as shown in the previous example. (I've separated each group with a blank line for clarity; it doesn't impact the rendering.) The dl entry in this chapter elaborates on these and other configurations, definition lists in general, and the role of dd.

User agents typically render a definition list by default like so (although you can change it with CSS):

Gold medal winner
    Jesse Owens (USA)
Silver medal winner
    Ralph Metcalfe (USA)
Bronze medal winner
    Tinus Osendarp (NED)

dl

A definition list

Syntax `<dl>`
    `<dt></dt>`
    `<dd></dd>`

    . . .

`</dl>`

Attributes Core, I18n, Events, *HTML5 Only:* Global

Description

Use the *definition list* (dl) to define a term (represented by one or more dt elements) and its description (represented by one or more dd elements). The dt may contain inline content only, while a dd may contain block-level content.

Though it's a natural fit for defining words like in a dictionary, the dl is not constrained to such narrow usage. As you will see, there is some levity concerning what constitutes a term and a description, as well as differing opinions about what is "legal."

note **Avoid using a dl to mark up dialogue (see the "When Can You Use a Definition List? HTML 4 Murkiness and HTML5 Clarification" box for more information).**

The following are several examples of how to use a definition list.

Example 1:

```
<dl>
    <dt>Boris Karloff</dt>
    <dd>Best known for his role in <cite>Frankenstein</cite>
    and related horror films, this scaremaster's real name
    was William Henry Pratt.</dd>

    . . .
</dl>
```

> **note** A definition list need not have more than one dt and dd group to constitute a list.

Example 1 is a basic dl. All of the following arrangements are valid for a group of dt and dd elements within a dl:

- A single dt grouped with a single dd, as in the previous Example 1 and as *Director* in the following Example 2. This is the most common occurrence.

- A single dt grouped with multiple dds. See *Writers* in Example 2.

- Multiple dts grouped with a single dd. See Example 3.

- Multiple dts grouped with multiple dds. See the note that follows Example 3.

Example 2 shows the first two of these by way of a list of credits for the movie *Amélie* (for all you French movie fanatics). It also demonstrates how to use a nested definition list.

Example 2:

```html
<h3>Credits for <cite>Am&eacute;lie</cite></h3>
<dl>
    <dt>Director</dt> <!-- Single dt with single dd -->
    <dd>Jean-Pierre Jeunet</dd>

    <dt>Writers</dt> <!-- Single dt with multiple dds -->
    <dd>Guillaume Laurant (story, screenplay)</dd>
    <dd>Jean-Pierre Jeunet (story)</dd>

    <dt>Cast</dt>
    <dd>
       <!-- Start nested list -->
       <dl>
          <dt>Audrey Tautou</dt> <!-- Actor/Actress -->
          <dd>Am&eacute;lie Poulain</dd> <!-- Character -->

          <dt>Mathieu Kassovitz</dt>
          <dd>Nino Quincampoix</dd>

          . . .
       </dl>
       <!-- end nested list -->
    </dd>
    . . .
</dl>
```

> **note** I included the blank line between each group of dt and dd elements so you could see the groupings more explicitly. It's not required in a definition list and doesn't impact its rendering in a user agent, so it's entirely up to you as an HTML author whether to include it.

User agents typically render a definition list by default as shown next (but you can alter it with CSS). Note how the dd text in the nested list is indented another step.

Director
    Jean-Pierre Jeunet
Writers
    Guillaume Laurant (story, screenplay)
    Jean-Pierre Jeunet (story)
Cast
    Audrey Tautou
        Amélie Poulain
    Mathieu Kassovitz
        Nino Quincampoix

Now let's look at another example. Although you shouldn't repeat the same dt *value* in a dl (for example, *Writers* appears only once in the previous example), you may have multiple dts grouped with a single dd, as I mentioned earlier.

Example 3:

```
<h2>Defining words with multiple spellings</h2>
<dl>
    <dt><dfn>bogeyman</dfn>, n.</dt> <!-- Multiple dts with
    single dd -->
    <dt><dfn>boogeyman</dfn>, n.</dt>
    <dd>A mythical creature that lurks under the beds of small
    children.</dd>
```

```
    <dt><dfn lang="en-gb">aluminium</dfn>, n.</dt>
    <dt><dfn>aluminum</dfn>, n.</dt>

    . . .
</dl>
```

 Notice that I used the lang attribute here to denote that *aluminium* is in the British version of English.

This example uses a definition list to define terms like in a dictionary (the most traditional use for a dl). You'll notice I wrapped the terms in a dfn element. You might think this is redundant, but it can be appropriate if it's consistent with the proper usage of dfn. (Please see the dfn entry in Chapter 5 for more details.) This approach is encouraged by HTML5 as a way to distinguish a dl used to define words in dictionary or glossary format from a dl used for other appropriate means like our movie credits. Although you're unlikely to find references to this approach elsewhere for HTML 4, too, I think it's appropriate.

note **An example of multiple dts grouped with multiple dds would be if in Example 3 *bogeyman/boogeyman* had a second definition. See the dt entry in this chapter for a related example.**

Deprecated Attributes

- compact: *Obsolete in HTML5*. This attribute is presentational in nature so was deprecated in favor of using CSS. Please see the ol entry in this chapter for more information.

When Can You Use a Definition List? HTML 4 Murkiness and HTML5 Clarification

HTML 4 has been criticized, and rightfully so, for being a little unclear in its definition of the definition list. Ironic, yes. As a result, the dl's use has been open to interpretation.

Purists argue that it should be used only for defining terms like in a dictionary or glossary. However, HTML 4 does not define the dl so strictly. It opens the door to other uses by referring to the dd as a "description" rather than a "definition" and by presenting an alternative usage for marking up dialogue, though most agree that application is ill-advised. (I don't recommend it, and HTML5 doesn't allow it; please also see the "HTML5, the dl Element, and Dialogue" box).

Others—what seems like the majority—think the concept of the term–description relationship is not intended to be quite so rigid and is an appropriate semantic choice for marking up other content if in context, such as the earlier movie credits example.

No HTML specification will be able to account for every use case for structuring content, at least not to everyone's satisfaction. For the most part, the ways in which developers have used the definition list beyond dictionary-like definitions arose from a desire to use semantic markup in cases where a better alternative was lacking. HTML5 recognizes this as well, providing a handful of example usages that range from glossary definitions to author–editor listings to meta information and more.

So, how far do you go with a definition list? My advice is to always consider the intent of a dl—defining content that has a term–description relationship. Use your best judgment to determine whether your content fits this model.

Unlike the other list types, the li element may not be part of a definition list unless it is part of an ordered or unordered list nested in a dd.

HTML5, the dl Element, and Dialogue

As noted in the previous box, HTML 4 declares that a dl may also be used to mark up dialogue, such as from a play. Despite the W3C's endorsement, this usage has not gained widespread approval from the development community, because many think it deviates too far from the intent of a definition list. Indeed, HTML5 acknowledges this by explicitly declaring that "The dl element is inappropriate for marking up dialogue."

Still, there isn't a perfect solution for dialogue in either HTML 4 or HTML5. The recommendation in HTML5 involving b and span is questionable and has already received pushback from some in the community. Those concerns and a proposed alternative (with its own issues) are discussed at *http://24ways.org/2009/incite-a-riot*.

dt

A definition list term

Syntax <dt></dt>

Attributes Core, I18n, Events, *HTML5 Only:* Global

Description

Use the dt element to denote a term in a definition list (dl). The term is described by at least one corresponding dd element that follows the dt. Please note that a dt may contain inline content only.

The simplest arrangement within a dl is one dt (term) grouped with one dd (description). Another possibility is shown in the following example, with one dt associated with multiple dds since *director* can be defined in many ways. The dl entry in this chapter elaborates on these and other configurations, definition lists in general, and the role of dt.

Example:

```
<dl>
    <dt><dfn>director</dfn></dt>
    <dd>One who directs</dd>
    <dd>One who oversees a group or an organization</dd>
    <dd>One who leads all aspects of the creation of a film</
➥ dd>
    . . .
</dl>
```

Most user agents typically render a definition list by default as shown here, except for the italics on *director*, which is because of the dfn element:

director
> One who directs
> One who oversees a group or an organization
> One who leads all aspects of the creation of a film

tip You might be wondering why *director* is wrapped in a dfn element. Isn't the dt sufficient to indicate it's a term? It depends on the context. Yes, a dt does denote a term, but a dfn has a more specific meaning, and in the context of a dt, dfn indicates the list is defining terms like a dictionary or glossary does. Please see the dl entry in this chapter and the dfn entry in Chapter 5 for more information and examples.

li

A list item

Syntax <li></li>

Attributes Core, I18n, Events, *HTML5 Only:* Global

Description

Use the li element to specify each list item in both ordered and unordered lists. It cannot be used on its own or in an element besides an ol or ul (or menu in HTML5). An li may contain both block-level and inline content, including div, span, a, p, all other list types, and more.

Examples:

```
<h4>Sequence of Events before Heading out Tonight</h4>
<ol>
        <li>Stretch</li>
        <li>Run five miles</li>
        <li>Shower and dress for dinner</li>
</ol>

<h4>Items to Buy for First Grade</h4>
<ul>
        <li>Notebooks</li>
        <li>Pencils</li>
        <li>Eraser</li>
</ul>
```

Please see the ol and ul entries in this chapter for more information about li for each list type.

Deprecated Attributes

The following attributes are deprecated in X/HTML:

- **type:** *Obsolete in HTML5.* This attribute is presentational in nature so was deprecated in favor of using CSS. Please see the ol entry in this chapter for more.

- **value:** There is no equivalent replacement in X/HTML. Please see the "HTML5 and the li Element" box for more information regarding HTML5.

HTML5 and the li Element

HTML5 reintroduces the value attribute and includes a new element, menu, that uses li.

ATTRIBUTES IN DETAIL

- **value="*number*":** The value attribute, which is deprecated in HTML 4, is a valid attribute in HTML5 as long as the li is a child of an ol. In this context, value specifies the ordinal value of its list item and adjusts the value of each subsequent item accordingly. Its value must be a valid integer.

  For instance, imagine a list of results in which there is a tie for third place.

  Example:

  ```
  <h3>Class President Voting Results</h3>
  <ol>
      <li>Hannah Carson (64)</li>
      <li>Stefan Rios (51)</li>
      <li>Kyla Wong (47)</li>
  ```
  (continues on next page)

HTML5 and the li Element (continued)

```
    <li value="3">Delores Cardinal (47)</li>
    <li>Michael McMurtry (44)</li>
</ol>
```

This list renders as follows:

1. Hannah Carson (64)
2. Stefan Rios (51)
3. Kyla Wong (47)
3. Delores Cardinal (47)
4. Michael McMurtry (44)

Notice that both the third and fourth items are numbered "3."
and the fifth item is numbered "4." The same principle applies if
you define your list markers as non-numeric values with CSS. For
example, with list-style-type: upper-roman; set, our example
would show "iii." twice, followed by "iv."

THE MENU ELEMENT

li is an optional child of the new menu element and is not wrapped
in either an ol or an ul in this context. Please see the menu entry in
Chapter 15 for more information.

ol

An ordered list

Syntax `<ol>`
    `<li></li>`
    . . .
    `</ol>`

Attributes Core, I18n, Events, *HTML5 Only:* Global

Description

Use an *ordered list* (ol) to define a list of items for which the sequence is important to the list's meaning. For example, you might want to list a ranking of your favorite songs, detail the steps in a recipe, or provide driving directions from one point to another. Each list item is represented by a li element, which can contain either block-level or inline content.

Example:

```
<h2>Directions to Birthday Party from Town Hall</h2>
<ol>
   <li>Head north on Hill Street for a quarter mile.</li>
   <li>Bear right at the fork onto Elm Street and continue
   for a mile.</li>
   <li>Turn left onto Glass Drive; it's the last house on the
   left.</li>
</ol>
```

Typically, most user agents render a number as the default marker before each list item, like so:

1. Head north on Hill Street for a quarter mile.
2. Bear right at the fork onto Elm Street and continue for a mile.
3. Turn left onto Glass Drive; it's the last house on the left.

You can control what type of marker appears with the list-style-type CSS property (don't use the deprecated HTML type attribute). Options include letters, Roman numerals, bullets (yes, even on an ordered list, though it isn't recommended), images, no marker at all, and more. If you're curious about the options, the CSS 2.1 Specification details them at *http://www.w3.org/TR/CSS21/generate.html#lists*.

As with definition lists (dl) and unordered lists (ul), you may nest all types of lists inside an ordered list, and vice versa. Please see the "Nested Lists" section earlier in this chapter for more information about nesting and an example using ordered lists.

Most important, remember to use an ol only if it's appropriate to describe the semantics of your content, not just because you want numbers or another sequenced marker before your content (though the two typically go hand in hand).

tip **I found this handy tip online. A good way to determine whether an ordered list or an unordered list is the correct semantic choice is to ask yourself whether the meaning of your list would change if you shuffled the items around. If the answer is yes, use an ol. Please see the dl and ul entries in this chapter for information about other list types.**

Recommended Uses

Aside from some of the obvious uses I've noted, an ordered list is the proper choice for marking up both breadcrumb and pagination navigation.

Breadcrumb navigation. Breadcrumb navigation is the series of links you'll often see above the content on, say, an e-commerce site to indicate the navigation path to the page you're viewing. A breadcrumb is often displayed like this example, with the page you're on displayed but not linked:

<u>Home</u> > <u>Products</u> > <u>Outdoors</u> > The Garden Weasel

An ordered list makes sense for this because a breadcrumb represents a distinct sequence of links.

Pagination navigation. Pagination navigation is the horizontal list of mostly numeric links you're probably used to seeing on e-commerce and news sites, allowing you to paginate through lists of products or to additional pages within an article.

> **tip** You can turn off the markers in your CSS with this:
> ```
> ol {
>     list-style-type: none;
> }
> ```

Deprecated Attributes

The following attributes are deprecated in X/HTML. Where applicable, I've described the method that has replaced the attribute and that replicates its purpose.

- compact: *Obsolete in HTML5.* Since this attribute is presentational in nature (and never gained wide support anyway), use the CSS margin, padding, and line-height CSS properties instead to adjust the spacing between list items and make the list more compact.

- **start**: Please see the "HTML5 and the ol Element" box for more information.

- **type**: *Obsolete in HTML5*. As noted earlier in the chapter, use the CSS `list-style-type` property instead of the `type` attribute to control each list item's marker styling. For instance, the following rule dictates that all ordered lists display an uppercase Roman numeral before each list item:

```
ol {
    list-style-type: upper-roman;
}
```

HTML5 and the ol Element

HTML5 defines two additional attributes for ordered lists: `start` and `reversed`.

ATTRIBUTES IN DETAIL

- **start="*number*"**: The `start` attribute, which is deprecated in HTML 4, is a valid attribute in HTML5. `start` specifies that an ordered list begins at a number (or non-numeric character depending on your style sheet) other than the default, which is "1." Its value must be a valid integer, even if the marker type you've specified in your CSS is not numeric, like `upper-roman`, shown earlier. For example, `start="4"` would display as "IV."

Example:

```
<ol start="5">
    <li>Preheat oven to 350 degrees</li>
    <li>Grease pan</li>
    <li>Mix ingredients in a large bowl</li>
</ol>
```

(continues on next page)

HTML5 and the ol Element (continued)

This renders as follows:

    5. Preheat oven to 350 degrees
    6. Grease pan
    7. Mix ingredients in a large bowl

If you had specified your marker as lower-roman, then it would begin with "v." instead.

- **reversed**: HTML5 introduces the new reversed Boolean attribute, which you use to indicate a descending list. (See "Attributes" in Chapter 1 for more about Boolean attributes.)

Example:

```
<h2>Countdown of the World's Three Coldest Locations</h2>
<ol reversed="reversed">
    <li>Oymyakon, Russia</li>
    <li>Plateau Station, Antarctica</li>
    <li>Vostok, Antarctica</li>
</ol>
<p><cite>http://www.aneki.com/coldest.html</cite></p>
```

This list renders as follows:

    3. Oymyakon, Russia
    2. Plateau Station, Antarctica
    1. Vostok, Antarctica

The XHTML5 syntax is <ol reversed="reversed">. You may use it in HTML5 documents as well if you prefer it over HTML5's <ol reversed> shortened format.

Please also see the li entry in this chapter for a discussion of the related value attribute.

ul

An unordered list

Syntax `<ul>`
            `<li></li>`
                `. . .`
            `</ul>`

Attributes Core, I18n, Events, *HTML5 Only:* Global

Description

Use an *unordered list* (ul) to define a generic list for which the sequence of items is not important. Each list item is represented by a li element, which can contain either block-level or inline content.

The ul is on the short list of the most commonly used elements on the Web because it is semantically appropriate for a wide variety of content (see "Recommended Uses").

Let's take a look at a simple example in the form of a shopping list.

Example:

```
<ul>
    <li>A bag of flour</li>
    <li>Carrots</li>
    <li>Fresh fruit</li>
</ul>
```

Typically, most user agents render a bullet before each list item by default, like so:

- A bag of flour
- Carrots
- Fresh fruit

However, the fact that a list may have bullets isn't important; it's whether your content calls for an unordered list semantically. CSS provides you full control over the formatting, allowing different types of bullets, images, no marker at all, and more.

> **tip** You can make sequential numbers appear as list item markers with this:
> ```
> ul {
>     list-style: decimal;
> }
> ```
> Use this only if your content is appropriate for an unordered list and not an ordered list. For example, you might post a list with the heading "Ten Tofu Dishes I Can't Live Without (in no particular order)," and you want to show decimals to reinforce that the list does, in fact, include ten items.

> **tip** I found this handy tip online. To determine whether an ordered list or an unordered list is the best semantic choice, ask yourself whether the meaning of your list would change if you shuffled the items around. If the answer is no, use a ul; otherwise, use an ol.

Recommended Uses

Here are just a few of the many ways in which unordered lists are utilized:

Navigation. Whether it's for global navigation, a group of footer links, or anywhere in between, the ul is the *de facto* standard for marking up site navigation. (Please see the ol entry for a couple exceptions.)

Tabs. This form of navigation typically appears across the top of a module.

Product grids and carousels. These are typically displayed horizontally.

Article headline lists. These often appear on a home page to surface links to recent articles or on an article subpage as related links. View source on your favorite news sites, and you're likely to see groups of links to articles formatted in a ul.

Related video lists. These typically have a thumbnail image and a title and description.

Deprecated Attributes

- compact and type: *Obsolete in HTML5*. These attribute are presentational in nature so were deprecated in favor of using CSS. Please see the ol entry in this chapter for more information.

Text

On the Web, content is king, and in most cases your content is text.

This chapter focuses on the elements used to mark up your carefully crafted prose, links, code samples, references, and more in order to enrich the semantics of your content. That, in turn, pleases both screen readers and search engines, and it affords you presentational control over your content via CSS.

As you'll see, there are *a lot* of elements covered in this chapter. You'll likely use only a handful regularly—such as a, p, em, and strong—but I really encourage you to become familiar with the others. You may find there are some elements you should have been using all along. cite is just one example of a hidden gem. And if you're working on an HTML5 site, be sure to check out this chapter's companion, Chapter 12, which focuses on text elements unique to HTML5.

a

An anchor

Syntax `<a></a>`

Attributes Core, I18n, Events, accesskey, charset*, coords*, href, hreflang, name*, rel, rev*, shape*, tabindex, target*, type, *HTML5 Only*: Global

Description

The a ("anchor") element is essential to the Web, providing the means to create a hyperlink to another page or serve as an anchor within a page to which a hyperlink points. You may wrap an a element around text or an image but not around a block level element, such as a p or div (this *is* allowed in HTML5, though; see the "HTML5 and the a element" box).

You may link *to* a variety of resources: another page (.html, .php, and so on), an anchor within a page, a document such as a PDF, an image, an e-mail address, and more. The href attribute provides the link path and takes on many forms.

Example 1 (simple link to another resource):

```
<!-- link within the same folder -->
<p>Africa has numerous inspiring areas to <a href="parks-and-
➥ reserves.html">experience animals in the wild</a>.</p>

<!-- link to another site -->
<p>. . . <a href="http://en.wikipedia.org/wiki/Norway"
title="History, geography, culture and more">Norway on
Wikipedia</a> . . .</p>
```

The optional title attribute typically displays as a tooltip and may be read by a screen reader. As you no doubt know, browsers underline and display links in a different color than static text by default, like so:

Africa has numerous inspiring areas to <u>experience animals in the wild</u>.

For simplicity's sake, I'll show only the a element in most of the remaining examples, but in practice, be sure each one is wrapped in a block-level element, such as a p.

Drill down from the current page location to a subfolder by including the proper path. Example 2 drills down to products and then to shoes.

Example 2 (link to subpage):

```
. . . <a href="products/shoes/basketball.html">basketball
shoes</a> . . .
```

Conversely, use ../ to link to a resource one folder level up from the current page. If you use ../../, the link points two levels up, and so on.

Example 3 (link up a level or two):

```
. . . <a href="../ozzie.html">Pictures of Ozzie</a> . . .

<!-- Up two levels and down one -->
. . . <a href="../../organic/salads.html"><img src="salad.jpg"
width="200" height="200" alt="organic salad" /></a> . . .
```

Each of those examples (except the one linking to Wikipedia) has a *relative path*, meaning they are relative to the location of the linking document. Although you can link throughout your site with those methods, an *absolute path* is often your best choice. It begins with /, which points to the site's root, and then you drill down from there. Consequently, it doesn't matter where the linking document lives in the directory hierarchy, because the link will always work.

For instance, the page containing the link in Example 4 could be one level deep or a dozen, but the link would be the same.

Example 4 (link with absolute path):

```
. . . <a href="/products/shoes/basketball.html">basketball
shoes</a> . . .
```

Linking to an e-mail address is equally simple. Just prefix the e-mail address with mailto:. The link will open the user's e-mail client if he or she has one installed and populate the To: field with the address.

Example 5 (link to e-mail address):

```
. . . <a href="mailto:slee@yourdomain.com">contact Sean Lee
⮕ </a> . . .
```

If you define an anchor or element with id="cheetahs", you may link directly to that portion of the page by assigning # plus the id to the href, as in Example 6. (To link to an anchor on another page, include the file-name, as in href="big-cats.html#cheetahs".)

Example 6 (link to anchor):

```
<!-- links from here -->
<p>Visit Africa to <a href="#cheetahs">experience cheetahs in
the wild</a>.</p>

<!-- to here in the current document (Approach #1) -->
. . .
<h2><a href="#cheetahs" id="cheetahs"></a>Experience Cheetahs
⮕ </h2>

. . .
```

This is an alternative approach:

```
<!-- to here in the current document (Approach #2) -->
. . .
<h2 id="cheetahs">Experience Cheetahs</h2>
. . .
```

Both approaches work across browsers—the page jumps to that point—but neither is perfect from a usability standpoint. In the second one, if you navigate with the Tab key in Internet Explorer after navigating to the h2, it jumps you to the first link *on the page* rather than the first link after the h2.

The first approach, although a little cumbersome, ensures Internet Explorer's tabbing order continues from the anchor as most users would expect. But, it adds a link that does nothing. (Note you could also wrap the link around "Experience Cheetahs.")

Meanwhile, Chrome's tabbing misbehaves regardless, depending on your point of view. It ignores your current position in the page, so pressing Tab takes you to the first link after the last one you activated, not after the id anchor to which you've jumped.

Attributes in Detail

All flavors of HTML share the following *a* attributes unless otherwise noted. (Please see the "HTML5 and the *a* Element" box for additional attributes specific to HTML5.)

- **accesskey**: Please see "Attributes" in Chapter 1 for details.

- **charset**: *Obsolete in HTML5.* This specifies the character encoding of the link destination. Please see "Character Encoding" in Chapter 1 for more details. This is typically omitted.

- **coords and shape**: *Obsolete in HTML5*. These two attributes define a client-side image map that uses the object element. However, browser support of object client-side image maps is extremely poor (Firefox and Opera 9.2 and newer only), so use the map element instead (please see map in Chapter 6).

- **href="*uri*"**: The most powerful attribute on the Web, href defines the link destination. Please see the previous examples.

- **hreflang="*langcode*"**: This indicates the base language of the href's destination, much in the way the lang attribute specifies the language of other HTML elements. Hence, you may use hreflang only when href is present.

- **name="*cdata*"**: *Deprecated in XHTML but validates. *Obsolete in HTML5*. This provides the anchor with a unique name so you can link to it from another a. It must be unique within a page, and it shares a namespace with id. The name attribute is a vestige of earlier versions of HTML, and id has replaced it as the attribute to use (see Example 6).

- **rel="*link-types*" and rev="*link-types*"**: *rev is obsolete in HTML5*. rel and rev have opposite meanings and are used in conjunction with href. The rel attribute indicates the relationship from the current document to the linked resource. rev ("reverse") indicates the relationship from the linked resource to the current document; historically, it's been misunderstood and rarely used, which is why it's not included in HTML5. The following examples illustrate their differences:

```
<!-- rel specifies that 04-giraffes.html is a chapter of
the book of which the current document is a part -->
<p>Learn that and more in <a href="04-giraffes.html"
rel="chapter">Giraffes</a>.</p>

<!-- rev specifies that the current page is an appendix,
NOT that chapter-14.html is -->
```

```
<p>As stated earlier, <a href="chapter-14.html"
rev="appendix">tofu is delicious</a>.</p>
```

Each rel and rev value must be a space-separated list. For instance, in the previous example, rel="chapter section" would indicate the href points to a section within a chapter. Please see "Link Types" in Chapter 1 for the list of defined values.

You do not have to include rel or rev on each anchor (including one or both is far less common than not), because if either is undefined, is left blank, or contains a value the user agent doesn't recognize, no relationship is defined. The link still functions, though.

- **tabindex**: Please see "Attributes" in Chapter 1 for details.
- **target**: *Not valid with Strict X/HTML DOCTYPEs*. target specifies the name of the frame or iframe in which the link should open. If the name doesn't exist, the link opens in a window. HTML provides four special target names with specific behavior: _blank (link opens in a new, unnamed window), _self, _parent, and _top. Please see the frameset element in Chapter 10 for more details. target is not deprecated in HTML5, but it may not reference a frame element since frames don't exist in HTML5.

Beginning authors often wonder how to open a link in a new window while using a Strict DOCTYPE, since target isn't allowed. Let me preface this by saying that it's best *not* to open a link in a new window, because you want to leave that decision up to the user. But for those times when you must, you can implement it with JavaScript. One approach uses rel="external" on the a as a hook for the script. You can find JavaScript for it by searching online. No matter your method, I recommend you add title="Opens external site in new window" or a similar message to each relevant link as a cue to users. Additionally, use CSS to place an icon next to each link so users know at a glance the link behaves differently.

- **type="*content-type*"**: Tells the user agent the content type of the content at the link's destination. It is only advisory.

HTML5 and the *a* element

HTML5 introduces a few changes to the *a* element.

a as Placeholder

If *a* doesn't have the href attribute, it represents a link placeholder. For example, you could populate the *a* dynamically with JavaScript based on user behavior.

Wrap *a* Around Nearly Any Element

In a big and extremely useful departure from previous versions of HTML, HTML5 allows wrapping an *a* around most elements, including paragraphs, lists, and more. For example, the following is valid HTML5, making both the h1 and h2 text an active link:

```
<a href="giraffe-escapes.html">
    <hgroup>
        <h1>Giraffe Escapes from Zoo</h1>
        <h2>Animals worldwide rejoice</h2>
    </hgroup>
</a>
```

The only limitation is that *a* cannot contain elements classified as interactive content, such as other links, the audio, video, details, form, iframe elements, and more (they're mostly common sense). The validator will tell you when you've gone astray.

(continues on next page)

HTML5 and the *a* element (continued)

Attributes in Detail

HTML5 includes these additional attributes:

- **media**: This attribute describes the media for which the href destination resource was designed (just like the media attribute when using link to load a style sheet). It is only advisory. The value is "all" if media is omitted; otherwise, it must be a valid media query list from the Media Queries specification (*http://www.w3.org/TR/2009/CR-css3-mediaqueries-20090915/#syntax*). media is allowed only if href is present.

- **ping**: ping facilitates tracking user behavior to gather analytics. It specifies a space-separated list of URLs (one is fine, too) that the user agent should notify if the user follows a hyperlink. Typically, this would be a server-side script that logs the user's action. ping is allowed only if href is present.

    Historically, developers have used other tracking methods, but they're typically hidden from the user. User agents supporting ping allow one to disable it, putting tracking in control of the user where it belongs (if you're a marketer, you might disagree!). And ping improves performance by eliminating the additional overhead of other methods (some require more trips to the server and/or load extra JavaScript).

abbr

An abbreviation

Syntax <abbr></abbr>

Attributes Core, I18n, Events, *HTML5 Only:* Global

Description

Use the abbr element to mark up an abbreviation, such as *Jr.* for Junior, *UK* for United Kingdom, and *B.S.* for Bachelor of Science. abbr is often confused with the acronym element, which is also featured in this chapter. Please see *http://www.htmlfiver.com/extras/abbr-acronym/* for more discussion of the difference between the two.

Example 1:

```
<p>They wake up at 7 <abbr>a.m.</abbr> and go to bed at 9
<abbr>p.m.</abbr> every day.</p>

<p>They listen to games via the online <abbr title="Major
League Baseball">MLB</abbr> Gameday Audio service.</p>
```

Note the use of the optional title attribute to provide the expansion of the abbreviation. title improves accessibility, since a user can configure a screen reader to announce the text, and it also appears as a tooltip when the mouse pointer is on the abbr.

Alternatively, if you want to make the expansion even more accessible and explicit, as well as support printing it in all browsers, you can place it in parentheses instead of in the title, as shown in Example 2.

Example 2:

```
<p>They listen to games via the online <abbr>MLB</abbr>
(Major League Baseball) Gameday Audio service.</p>
```

Rendering of abbr and acronym

User agents typically don't display *abbr* or *acronym* text differently than other text by default, though some such as Firefox and Opera do show a dotted bottom border (underline) if you define a *title*. This acts as a visual cue to sighted users that a tooltip is available. You may replicate this effect in other modern browsers with this bit of CSS:

```
/* show underline when a title is provided */
abbr[title], acronym[title] {
    border-bottom-style: dotted;
    border-bottom-width: 1px;
}
```

note If you don't see the dotted bottom border on your *abbr* or *acronym* in Internet Explorer, try adjusting the parent element's `line-height` property in CSS.

note Internet Explorer 6 renders *abbr* text, but it doesn't recognize *abbr* as an element (unless you execute `document.createElement('abbr')` first), so you can't style it with CSS, and the `title` tooltip won't display.

HTML5 and the *abbr* Element

HTML5 eliminates the confusion between abbreviations and acronyms by declaring the *acronym* element obsolete and advising authors to use *abbr* in all instances.

It also specifies that if an abbreviation is in plural form within the element, the *title* text, if present, should be plural as well.

acronym

An acronym

Syntax `<acronym></acronym>`

Attributes Core, I18n, Events, *HTML5 Only:* Global

Description

The `acronym` element defines an acronym. It is often confused with the *abbr* element, which is for abbreviations. (An acronym is also an abbreviation but one that spells a word, such as *laser, radar,* and *scuba*.) Please see *http://www.htmlfiver.com/extras/abbr-acronym/* for more discussion of the difference between the two.

Example:

```
<p>After the <acronym>radar</acronym> detected movement under
the ship, she threw on her <acronym title="self-contained
underwater breathing apparatus">scuba</acronym> gear to go
check it out.</p>
```

As shown, the optional `title` attribute defines the expanded form of the acronym. Please see the *abbr* entry for more about the value of `title` and an alternative approach, as well as how `title` impacts `acronym` rendering in some browsers.

HTML5 and the acronym Element

HTML5 eliminates the confusion between abbreviations and acronyms by declaring the `acronym` element obsolete and advising authors to use *abbr* in all instances.

b

Bold text

Syntax `<b></b>`

Attributes Core, I18n, Events, *HTML5 Only:* Global

Description

In X/HTML, the b element is purely presentational; it renders text as bold but provides no meaning. You can think of it as a span element that is bold by default. Because it's solely presentational, b fell out of favor several years ago like the i element and is all but deprecated in the eyes of many. Developers are advised to use the strong element instead whenever appropriate, since it has semantic value and doesn't speak to how the enclosed text should look.

Example:

```
<!-- Uses strong instead of b -->
<p>That intersection is <strong>extremely dangerous
➥ </strong>.</p>
```

User agents render both strong and b the same way by default (and both can be altered with CSS):

That intersection is **extremely dangerous**.

However, don't use strong for content, such as a heading, just because you want it to be bold. Instead, use h1–h6, or the appropriate semantic element and style it accordingly with CSS.

b vs. strong, HTML5, and More

HTML5 redefines b so its use is rooted in typographical conventions, instead of solely making text bold. Please see the i element entry in this chapter for more background concerning b vs. strong, as well as b's role in HTML5.

bdo

Bidirectional text override

Syntax `<bdo dir=""></bdo>`

Attributes Core (dir is required), *HTML5 Only:* Global

Description

Use the bdo ("bidirectional override") element and its required dir attribute to change the directionality of the enclosed text. dir specifies the desired display direction and takes a value of either ltr ("left to right") or rtl ("right to left").

Example 1:
```
<p>This text appears left-to-right by default, while
<bdo dir="rtl">this appears right-to-left</bdo>.</p>
```

User agents render this as follows:

This text appears left-to-right by default, while tfel-ot-thgir sraeppa siht.

That's a crude example just to show the basic concept, but here's some of the "why" and "when" of bdo.

Each Unicode character has a directionality associated with it—either left to right (like Latin characters in most languages) or right to left (like characters in Arabic or Hebrew). Unicode's bidirectional ("bidi") algorithm determines how to display content that includes a mixture of both left-to-right and right-to-left characters. bdo comes into play when the algorithm *doesn't* display the content as intended and you need to override it. Please see *http://www.htmlfiver.com/extras/bdo/* for more details. Additionally, the W3C's article "Creating HTML Pages in Arabic, Hebrew and Other Right-to-left Scripts" (*http://www.w3.org/International/tutorials/bidi-xhtml/*) discusses the issues at length.

big

Larger text

Syntax `<big></big>`

Attributes Core, I18n, Events, *HTML5 Only:* Global

Description

Text contained in a big element renders in an indeterminate larger size (and it may vary in user agents). Like the small element, big isn't officially deprecated in X/HTML, but practically speaking it is, and developers are advised never to use it. Instead, use CSS to control your font size in conjunction with a proper semantic element. The em and, especially, strong elements are ideal substitutes for cases in which you might have been inclined to use big. (Avoid using span since it has no semantic meaning and doesn't enhance accessibility.) Example 1 shows strong in place of big.

Example:

```
<p>This is the sale <strong>you CAN'T miss!</strong></p>
```

The strong text won't be larger than its surrounding text by default, but you can style it as you please with CSS: larger, a normal weight instead of the default bold, and so on.

HTML5 and the big element

The big element is obsolete in HTML5.

blockquote

A long quotation

Syntax `<blockquote></blockquote>`

Attributes Core, I18n, Events, cite, *HTML5 Only:* Global

Description

Use the blockquote element to denote a long (block-level) quotation. It is the counterpart to the q element, which is appropriate for a short (inline) quotation. The optional cite attribute allows you to specify the source's URI.

Example:

```
<p>In <cite>The Brothers Karamazov</cite>, Dostoevsky wrote:
➥ </p>
<blockquote cite="http://www.dostoevskybooks.com/the-brothers-
➥ karamazov/">
```

```
    <p>The stupider one is, the closer one is to reality. The
    stupider one is, the clearer one is. Stupidity is brief
    and artless, while intelligence wriggles and hides
    itself. Intelligence is a knave, but stupidity is honest
    and straightforward.</p>
</blockquote>
```

Browsers typically indent blockquote content by default (you can change this with CSS):

In *The Brothers Karamazov*, Dostoevsky wrote:

> The stupider one is, the closer one is to reality. The stupider one is, the clearer one is. Stupidity is brief and artless, while intelligence wriggles and hides itself. Intelligence is a knave, but stupidity is honest and straightforward.

note Be sure to use blockquote only if your content is quoted from a source, not just because you want to indent it. You may indent other HTML elements by setting the margin-left property in CSS.

Attributes in Detail

- **cite**: Use this optional attribute to include a URI that points to the quotation's source. The previous example refers to Dostoevsky's book on a site (fictitious, in this case). Please see the dfn element entry in this chapter for more details about cite accessibility and presentation issues. (Note: The cite attribute is different from the cite element, which is also used in the example and described in full in this chapter.)

note For a page with a Strict DOCTYPE, blockquote content must be marked up with the appropriate elements (like p in the example) rather than wrapped directly. However, I strongly encourage you to mark it up even if you're using a Transitional DOCTYPE. It's better for accessibility and controlling presentation with CSS, and it'll make your transition to Strict easier.

HTML5 and the blockquote Element

HTML5 says the blockquote and cite elements are invalid for representing a conversation.

---

br

A line break

Syntax
 or

Attributes Core, I18n, Events, *HTML5 Only:* Global

Description

The br element forces a line break in a run of text, such as in a poem or street address. As a rule, use br sparingly since it mixes presentation (the domain of CSS) with your HTML. Do *not* use it to create a break between paragraphs; wrap the content in the p element instead, and define the space between paragraphs with the CSS margin property.

Example:

```
<p>
    125 Center Street<br />
    Moose Jaw, Saskatchewan<br />
    Canada S6H 3J9
</p>
```

Deprecated Attributes

- **clear**: Use the CSS clear property instead to dictate the flow of content that follows a br.

cite

A reference to a source

Syntax `<cite></cite>`

Attributes Core, I18n, Events, *HTML5 Only:* Global

Description

Use the `cite` element for a citation or reference to a source. Examples
include the title of a play, a script, a book, a song, a movie, a photo, a
sculpture, a concert or musical tour, a specification, a newspaper, a legal
paper, a person, and more.

For instances in which you are quoting from the cited source, use `q` or
`blockquote`, as appropriate, to mark up the quoted text (please see
their entries in this chapter). To be clear, `cite` is only for the source, not
what you are quoting from it. `cite` may also be used without a related
quotation.

Examples:

```
<p>Two of the books on her summer reading list are <cite>A
Separate Peace</cite> and <cite>The Odyssey</cite>.</p>

<p>Which character in <cite>This is Spinal Tap</cite> said,
<q>It's such a fine line between stupid, and clever</q>?</p>

<p>When he went to The Louvre, he learned that <cite>Mona
Lisa</cite> is also known as <cite>La Gioconda</cite>.</p>
```

User agents typically italicize `cite` text by default, like this (you can alter
it with CSS):

Which character in *This Is Spinal Tap* said, "It's such a fine line between stupid and clever"?

HTML 4, HTML5, and the `cite` Element Dustup

HTML 4 is different from HTML5 in that it also allows using `cite` on a person's name, such as when quoting the person. HTML 4 provides this example (I've changed the element names from uppercase to lowercase):

```
As <cite>Harry S. Truman</cite> said,
<q lang="en-us">The buck stops here.</q>
```

In addition to instances like that, developers often use `cite` for the name of blog and article commenters (the default WordPress theme does, too).

Amid some disagreement in the development community, HTML5 explicitly declares that using `cite` for a person's name is not appropriate. Instead, it defines `cite` as solely for the "title of a work," like a title of a play, a script, and the other ones (except a person) listed in the previous description. Many developers have made it clear they intend to continue to use `cite` on names because HTML5 doesn't provide an alternative they deem acceptable (namely, the `span` and `b` elements).

code

A code fragment

Syntax `<code></code>`

Attributes Core, I18n, Events, *HTML5 Only:* Global

Description

Use the code element to mark up a fragment of computer code. For instance, you'll often see code used on Web tutorials. Typically, it's nested in p or pre, as appropriate, though other elements may be acceptable, too.

Example:

```
<p>The <code>showPhoto(id)</code> function displays the
full-size photo of the thumbnail in our <code>&lt;
➥ ul id=&quot;thumbnails&quot;&gt;</code> carousel list.</p>
```

User agents typically render code in a monospace font by default, like so:

The **showPhoto(id)** function displays the full-size photo of the thumbnail in our **<ul id="thumbnails">** carousel list.

If you'd like to render a block of code, wrap it in a pre element to preserve its formatting. Please see the pre entry in this chapter for an example and more information.

 Please see the kbd, samp, and var element entries in this chapter for other computer- and programming-related semantics.

HTML5 and the code Element

HTML5 says code is also appropriate for a filename. HTML 4 is quite short on details about code, but in my judgment, this is appropriate for X/HTML usage, too.

del

Deleted content

Syntax `<del></del>`

Attributes Core, I18n, Events, `cite`, `datetime`, *HTML5 Only:* Global

Description

The del element indicates content that has been deleted from a previous version of the document. It's useful when you'd like to explicitly show what has changed as a page evolves. Its counterpart is the ins element, which indicates content that's been inserted since a previous version. You are not required to use them in tandem, however.

For both, think of a technical specification or legal document that goes through multiple iterations before becoming final, a gift registry list that is updated as items are purchased, or a Web tutorial you update after a reader provides valuable feedback in the comments section. In each case, you may want to inform the reader of the content's evolution with del and/or ins.

Example 1 (as inline element):

```
<h3>Tomorrow's Showtimes</h3>
<ol>
    <li><ins>2 <abbr>p.m.</abbr> (Another show just added!)
    ➥ </ins></li>
    <li><del datetime="2010-03-03T10:16:15-05:00">5 <abbr>p.m.
    ➥ </abbr></del> <ins>SOLD OUT</ins></li>
    <li><del cite="http://www.hot-ticket-plays.com/show-
    ➥ sells-quickly/" datetime="2010-03-02T10:10:14-05:00">8:30
    <abbr>p.m.</abbr></del> <ins>SOLD OUT</ins></li>
</ol>
```

By default, user agents typically render a strikethrough on del content
and underline ins content (you can alter this with CSS). Example 1 would
appear like this:

1. <ins>2 p.m. (Another show just added!)</ins>

2. ~~5 p.m.~~ <ins>SOLD OUT</ins>

3. ~~8:30 p.m.~~ <ins>SOLD OUT</ins>

As I mentioned, del and ins are often used together but don't have to be.
For example, I inserted content in the first list item but didn't delete any.
Conversely, there may be times you document a deletion without insert-
ing a replacement.

Attributes in Detail

These attributes have the same purpose for both del and ins:

- **cite="*url*"**: Use this optional attribute to include a URI to a source
  that explains why the change was made. For instance, in the last li
  in Example 1, cite might point to a story about the show selling out

in ten minutes. Alternatively, you could provide a brief message in the `title` attribute, which displays as a tooltip. (Note: The `cite` attribute is different from the `cite` element, which is also described in this chapter.)

- **datetime**: Use this optional attribute to specify the date and time of the change, as shown in Example 1. The required format is YYYY-MM-DDThh:mm:ssTZD. Please see *http://www.w3.org/TR/html4/types.html#type-datetime* for a full explanation.

note `cite` and `datetime` are curious in that they add value to your content, but browsers don't readily expose the information to users. Please see *http://www.htmlfiver.com/extras/del-ins/* for further discussion of this accessibility issue and some solutions.

As Inline or Block-Level Element

`del` and `ins` are rare in that they can be either inline or block-level elements. They are inline when surrounding content *within* a block-level element, such as a paragraph or the `li` in Example 1. They are block-level when they contain one or more block-level elements, as in Example 2. An instance of `del` or `ins` cannot be both at the same time, however; you cannot nest block-level content inside `del` or `ins` when either is used inline.

This example shows `ins` as a block-level element; the approach is the same for `del`.

Example 2 (as block-level element):

```
<ins>
    <p><strong>Update:</strong> Since initial publication of
    this story, we learned that Mr. Johnson's bike ride
    across the United States will commence on July 7th.</p>
</ins>
```

note Browsers render content in a block-level del and ins inconsistently by default. Most display a strikethrough for del and an underline for ins on all nested content as expected, but at the least, Firefox 3.5 and older do not. You can rectify this with the following explicit CSS rule (the * means every element inside del and ins gets the treatment):

```
del * {
    text-decoration: line-through;
}
ins * {
    text-decoration: underline;
}
```

dfn

Defining instance of term

Syntax <dfn></dfn>

Attributes Core, I18n, Events, *HTML5 Only:* Global

Description

The dfn element indicates the defining instance of a term. Wrap dfn only around the term you're defining, not the definition itself.

Example 1:

```
<p>The contestant was asked to spell &ldquo;pleonasm.&rdquo;
She asked for the definition and was told that <dfn>pleonasm
➥ </dfn> means <q>a redundant word or expression</q> (Ref:
<cite><a href="http://dictionary.reference.com/browse/
➥ pleonasm">dictionary.com</a></cite>).</p>
```

User agents typically italicize dfn text by default:

The contestant was asked to spell "pleonasm." She asked for the definition and was told that *pleonasm* means a redundant word or expression (Ref: *dictionary.com*).

Note that although *pleonasm* appears twice in our example, dfn marks the second one only, because that's when I defined the term (that is, it's the defining instance). Similarly, if I were to use *pleonasm* subsequently in the document, I wouldn't wrap it in dfn because I've already defined it. However, I could add an id to the dfn and link to it from other points in the document or site. Please also note that you don't need to use the cite element each time you use dfn, just when you reference a source.

dfn may also enclose another inline element like abbr, when appropriate.

Example 2:

```
<p>A <dfn><abbr title="Junior">Jr.</abbr></dfn> is a son who
has the same full name as his father.</p>
```

 dfn is also appropriate in a definition list. Please see the dl and dt elements in Chapter 4 for more details.

HTML5 and the dfn Element

HTML5 says, "The paragraph, description list group, or section that is the nearest ancestor of the dfn element must also contain the definition(s) for the term given by the dfn element." The previous paragraph examples reflect this.

HTML5 also stipulates that if you use the optional title attribute, it should be the same as the dfn term. However, if, as in Example 2, you nest a single abbr in dfn and the dfn does not have a text node of its own, the optional title should be on the abbr only.

em

Emphasize text

Syntax <em></em>

Attributes Core, I18n, Events, *HTML5 Only:* Global

Description

Use the em element to convey emphasis. Its counterpart is the strong element, which conveys greater emphasis. (Please see the "HTML5 and the em Element" box concerning differences in HTML5.)

Although both em and the i element render text in italics by default, always use em when emphasizing content since it has semantic meaning and i doesn't in X/HTML. Please see the i entry in this chapter for a detailed discussion about i vs. em.

Example:

<p>Your Ford Pinto is <em>really</em> cool.</p>

This typically displays by default as follows:

Your Ford Pinto is *really* cool.

You can change the display with CSS, of course, even making it bold if you'd like.

note It's not appropriate to use em simply as a means to italicize text. As always, choose the proper semantic element for your content and then style it. For instance, there may be times when the cite element is the right choice instead of em.

HTML5 and the em Element

In HTML 4, em is for emphasis, and the strong element is for greater emphasis. HTML5 redefines them a bit, so em accounts for all degrees of emphasis and strong conveys importance. It's a subtle shift.

In HTML5, em represents different levels of emphasis by whether it's nested in another em; each nested level is emphasized more than its parent. Here I've adjusted the previous example to demonstrate:

```
<p>Your Ford Pinto is <em><em>really</em> cool</em>.</p>
```

Now, I'm emphasizing both *really* and *cool*, but *really* is stronger because it's contained in the nested em.

HTML5 also reminds us that em changes the meaning of a sentence by where it appears. For instance, the next example conveys that "your" Pinto is really cool, while someone else's isn't.

```
<p><em>Your</em> Ford Pinto is really cool.</p>
```

As another example, if you were excited beyond belief by the Pinto, you could convey it by placing the entire sentence in an em and adding an optional exclamation mark to leave no doubt:

```
<p><em>Your Ford Pinto is really cool!</em></p>
```

i

Italicized text

Syntax `<i></i>`

Attributes Core, I18n, Events, *HTML5 Only:* Global

Description

In X/HTML, the i element is purely presentational; it renders text in italics but provides no meaning. You can think of it as a span element that is italicized by default. Because it's solely presentational, i fell out of favor several years ago like the b element. Use the em element instead to emphasize text, since it has semantic value and doesn't speak to how the enclosed text should look.

Example:

```
<!-- Uses em instead of i -->
<p>He had a great final kick, but <em>just</em> missed
catching the race leader.</p>
```

User agents render both em and i the same way (and both can be altered with CSS):

He had a great final kick, but *just* missed catching the race leader.

b and i vs. strong and em, a Little Background, and HTML5

The b and i elements were the subject of much opinionated discussion in the earlier days of HTML5's evolution. Some called for their deprecation or removal, while others thought they had to remain. Though a decision has been made, the sentiments haven't changed.

You could spend hours reading all angles of the arguments both for and against b and i, but they boil down to a couple key positions: Those against them think it's wrong to use an element strictly intended for presentation and that conveys no semantic meaning; those for them think b and i are too entrenched in the Web (many millions of pages use them) and believe em and strong are not appropriate semantics for every case.

To the latter, there are established typographic conventions in traditional publishing that fall between the cracks of the available HTML semantics. Among them are italicizing certain scientific names (for example, "The *Ulmus americana* is the Massachusetts state tree."), foreign phrases (for example, "The couple exhibited a *joie de vivre* that was infectious."), and named vehicles (for example, "The *Orient Express* began service in 1883."). These italicized terms aren't emphasized, just stylized per convention. There are fewer cases for bold, but HTML5 cites keywords in a document abstract and a product name in a review as examples.

Rather than create several new semantic elements (and further muddy the waters) to address cases like these, HTML5 takes a practical stance by trying to make do with what we have: em for all levels of emphasis, strong for importance, and b and i for the between-the-cracks cases to "stylistically offset [the text] from the normal prose." The notion is that although b and i don't carry explicit semantic meaning, the reader will recognize a difference is implied. And you're still free to change their appearance from bold and italics with CSS.

(continues on next page)

> ## b and i vs. strong and em,
> ## a Little Background, and HTML5 (continued)
>
> Make no mistake, though, HTML5 does emphasize that you use b
> and i only as a last resort when another element (such as strong, em,
> cite, and others) won't do.
>
> HTML5's approach is understandable, all things considered. That
> being said, the idea of always using em and strong instead of i and b,
> respectively, is so woven into the fabric of standards-focused devel-
> opers that the majority are unlikely to deviate. Many of them still
> think it is better to add some meaning to an element (such as with
> em), even if it isn't quite on point, than it is to use what they perceive
> to be a solely presentational element.

ins

Inserted content

Syntax `<ins></ins>`

Attributes Core, l18n, Events, cite, datetime, *HTML5 Only:* Global

Description

Use the ins element to denote content you've added to an HTML document since a previous version in cases when tracking the history adds
value. ins is often used in conjunction with the del element, which
denotes deleted content. As such, both elements and their attributes are
described in greater detail in the del entry in this chapter.

kbd

Text for user to enter

Syntax <kbd></kbd>

Attributes Core, I18n, Events, *HTML5 Only:* Global

Description

Use the kbd element to mark up text the user should enter. It applies to both letters typed and keys pressed.

Example:

```
<p>To log into the demo:</p>
<ol>
    <li>Type <kbd>tryDemo</kbd> in the User Name field</li>
    <li><kbd>TAB</kbd> to the Password field and type
<kbd>demoPass</kbd></li>
    <li>Hit <kbd>RETURN</kbd> or <kbd>ENTER</kbd></li>
</ol>
```

User agents typically display a monospace font for kbd by default. Our example (sans the paragraph) would render like this:

1. Type `tryDemo` in the User Name field

2. `TAB` to the Password field and type `demoPass`

3. Hit `RETURN` or `ENTER`

Please see the code, samp, and var elements for other computer- and programming-related semantics.

p

A paragraph

Syntax `<p></p>`

Attributes Core, l18n, Events, *HTML5 Only:* Global

Description

The p is one of the most-used elements on the Web, which should come as no surprise since its purpose is to define a paragraph.

You may use p on its own (see Example 1) or in conjunction with nested inline elements. For instance, you may see an img element in a paragraph, along with elements that enrich the semantics of the content, such as cite in Example 2.

Examples:

```
<p>Centuries-old sisters, Marge and Priscilla, were the
creation of the children's fertile imaginations.</p>
```

```
<p><img src="movie_poster.jpg" width="300" height="175"
alt="Monty Python and the Holy Grail poster" /><cite>Monty
Python and the Holy Grail</cite> was released in 1975.</p>
```

As shown here, browsers render each paragraph on its own line by default:

Centuries-old sisters, Marge and Priscilla, were the creation of the children's fertile imaginations.

. . . *next paragraph* . . .

Deprecated Attributes

- **align**: Use the CSS text-align property with a value of center, justify, left, or right instead.

 note Nesting a block-level element in a paragraph is not allowed.

pre

Preformatted text

Syntax <pre></pre>

Attributes Core, I18n, Events, *HTML5 Only:* Global

Description

Use the pre element to render preformatted text. The most common use case is to present a block of code, but you may also use pre for text and ASCII art.

Example 1 (code):

```
<pre>
   <code>
   var band = {
      bass: "Geddy",
      guitar: "Alex",
      drums: "Neil",
      showsPlayed: "2112"
   };
   </code>
</pre>
```

Browsers typically render this as shown (sans the outline) and in a monospace font:

```
var band = {
        bass: "Geddy",
        guitar: "Alex",
        drums: "Neil",
        showsPlayed: "2112"
};
```

As you see, pre preserves the indentation, so the code block displays in from the left edge. Without pre, the code displays like a sentence, making it harder to read even for our simple example:

```
var band = { bass: "Geddy", guitar: "Alex", drums:
"Neil", showsPlayed: "2112" };
```

Here is an example with text.

Example 2 (text):

```
<pre>
This is flush left.

              This begins fourteen spaces from the left side.


      This begins six spaces from the left side and two lines
↳ down.
</pre>
```

As expected, it displays just as it appears in the code (and as the content describes).

You'll notice that the paragraphs aren't wrapped in p elements. This is deliberate, because it's invalid to nest many HTML elements inside pre, including p, sub, sup, and more. Be sure to validate your pages to check whether you've accidentally included an invalid element in a pre.

Presentation Considerations with pre

Be aware that user agents typically disable automatic word wrapping of content inside a pre, so if it's too wide, it might affect your layout or force a horizontal scrollbar. The following CSS rule enables wrapping within pre in many browsers, but not Internet Explorer except version 8 when in IE8 mode.

```
pre {
    white-space: pre-wrap;
}
```

On a related note, in most cases I don't recommend you use white-space: pre; on an element such as div as a substitute for pre, because if the user agent doesn't support CSS, the formatting will be lost. Furthermore, the whitespace can be crucial to the semantics of the enclosed content, especially code, and only pre always preserves it.

Deprecated Attributes

- **width**: Use the CSS width property instead.

 note   pre isn't a shortcut for avoiding marking up your content with proper semantics and styling its presentation with CSS. For instance, if you want to post a news article you wrote in a word processor, don't simply copy and paste it into a pre if you like the spacing. Instead, wrap your content in p elements and write CSS as desired.

tip   Please see the code, kbd, samp, and var elements in his chapter for other computer- and programming-related semantics.

q

A short quotation

Syntax `<q></q>`

Attributes Core, l18n, Events, `cite`, *HTML5 Only:* Global

Use the q element to enclose a short (inline) quotation that doesn't require a paragraph break. The quotation may be a phrase someone said or a reference from a document, movie, song, and so on. q is the counterpart to the `blockquote` element, which is for long (block-level) quotations.

Example 1:

```
<p>Kathy is fond of quoting her favorite movie,
<cite>Phantasm</cite>, by exclaiming, <q cite="http://
➥www.phantasmscreenplay.com">You play a good game, boy, but
the game is finished!</q> every chance she gets.</p>
```

q can stand on its own or be paired with the `cite` element (in other words, `<cite>Phantasm</cite>`), as in Example 1.

Authors should not include quotation marks when they use q. Most user agents automatically render them as required by HTML 4 and HTML5. However, Internet Explorer 7 and older fail to do so. Here is the correct rendering:

Kathy is fond of quoting her favorite movie, **Phantasm**, by exclaiming, "You play a good game, boy, but the game is finished!" every chance she gets.

Be sure you don't use q simply because you want quotation marks around a word or phrase, though. For instance, `<p>He likes the word <q>morsel.</q></p>`, is improper because *morsel* isn't a quotation from a source. In that case, use character entities, such as `<p>He likes the word &ldquo;morsel.&rdquo;</p>` (or `&quot;` on each side for straight quotation marks).

Attributes in Detail

- **cite**: Use this optional attribute to include a URI to the source you are quoting. For instance, Example 1 points to the *Phantasm* screenplay on a site (fictitious, in this case). Please see the del element entry in this chapter for more details about cite accessibility and presentation issues. (Note that the cite attribute is different from the cite element, which is also used in Example 1 and described in full elsewhere in this chapter.)

Nested Quotations

You may also nest a q inside another one.

Example 2:

```
<p>The short story began, <q>When she was a child, she would
say, <q>Hello!</q> to everyone she passed.</q></p>
```

Since outer and inner quotations are treated differently in languages, add the lang attribute to q as needed. User agents are supposed to render Example 2 with single quotations around the nested portion, like this:

The short story began, "When she was a child, she would say, 'Hello!' to everyone she passed."

However, support is inconsistent (even with lang explicitly declared), including among modern browsers, surprisingly. Firefox handles it correctly, while the likes of Chrome and Safari render double quotations in all cases.

tip A handful of online tutorials discuss solutions for showing quotation marks for q across browsers consistently. Two examples are *http://monc.se/kitchen/129/rendering-quotes-with-css* and *http://juicystudio.com/article/fixing-ie-quotes.php*.

Because of the cross-browser issues, you may surround a quotation with a character entity such as “ (left quotation) and ” (right quotation) or " (straight quotation on each side) instead of using q. Similarly, ‘ and ’ render left and right single quotations, respectively. You do lose some of the semantics with this approach, though.

samp

Sample output text

Syntax <samp></samp>

Attributes Core, I18n, Events, *HTML5 Only:* Global

Description

The samp element represents sample output text from a program or script.

Example:

```
<p>Once the payment went through, the site returned a message
reading, <samp>Thanks for your order!</samp></p>
```

User agents typically display samp content in a monospace font by default, like this:

Once the payment went through, the site returned a message reading, `Thanks for your order!`

tip Please see the code, kbd, and var elements for other computer- and programming-related semantics.

small

Smaller text

Syntax `<small></small>`

Attributes Core, I18n, Events, *HTML5 Only:* Global

Description

Text contained in a `small` element renders in an indeterminate smaller size (and it may vary in user agents). Like the `big` element, `small` isn't officially deprecated in X/HTML, but practically speaking it is, and developers are advised never to use it (see the "HTML5 and the `small` Element" box for an exception). Instead, control your font size with CSS in conjunction with a proper semantic element. The `em` element is often a good substitute, as shown here.

Example:

```
<p>His handwriting was <em>very, very tiny</em>, so he was
able to fit a term's worth of notes on a single page.</p>
```

His handwriting was *very, very tiny*, so he was able to fit a term's worth of notes on a single page.

The `em` text won't be smaller than its surrounding text by default, but you can style it with CSS as you please. Use `span` in cases when `em` or another element doesn't feel appropriate for your content and you just need a container to facilitate making it smaller with CSS.

HTML5 and the small Element

HTML5 has redefined the small element to put it to use instead of making it obsolete like the big element.

According to HTML5, use small for side comments such as fine print, which "typically features disclaimers, caveats, legal restrictions, or copyrights. Small print is also sometimes used for attribution, or for satisfying licensing requirements."

small is intended for brief portions of inline text, not spanning multiple paragraphs or other elements.

Example:

```
<p>Order now and you'll receive free shipping. <small>
(Some restrictions may apply.)</small></p>
```

small should not be confused with the HTML5-only aside element, which may contain large blocks of content (some of which may include small elements). Please see the aside entry in Chapter 11 for more details.

Lastly, if you use small with em and strong, it doesn't diminish the weight of the meaning of those elements.

strong

Stronger text emphasis

Syntax `<strong></strong>`

Attributes Core, I18n, Events, *HTML5 Only:* Global

Description

Use the `strong` element to convey stronger emphasis than its counter-part, the `em` element. (Note: The meaning has changed in HTML5. Please see the "HTML5 and the `strong` Element" box.)

Although both `strong` and the `b` element render in bold by default, always use `strong` instead when conveying stronger emphasis since `b` is purely presentational and has no semantic meaning in X/HTML. Please see the `i` element entry in this chapter for a detailed discussion about `b` and `i` vs. `strong` and `em` in HTML5.

Examples:

`<p>They've been married for <strong>44 years</strong>!</p>`

`<p><strong>Warning:</strong> Pan will be hot.</p>`

`strong` typically renders by default like this:

They've been married for **44 years**!

You can change it with CSS, of course, even making it italicized if you'd like.

note   It's not appropriate to use `strong` simply as a means to bold text. As always, choose the proper semantics for your content and then style it. For instance, if you're tempted to use `strong` to create a heading, use the appropriate heading level (h1–h6) instead.

HTML5 and the strong Element

In X/HTML, em is for emphasis, and the strong element is for greater emphasis. HTML5 redefines them a bit, so em accounts for all degrees of emphasis and strong conveys importance. It's a subtle shift. The first example shown earlier (that is <p>They've been married . . .</p>) would use em in HTML5 instead of strong.

Additionally, in HTML5, strong indicates a greater level of importance each time it's nested in another strong. Let's suppose we wrap the entire second example in strong:

```
<p><strong><strong>Warning:</strong> Pan will be hot.
➥ </strong></p>
```

The inner strong, in other words, Warning:, conveys greater importance than the parent strong.

sub

A subscript

Syntax

Attributes   Core, I18n, Events, *HTML5 Only:* Global

Description

Use the sub element to mark up content suitable for subscript notation (in other words, not just because you want content to appear below the line of text).

Example:

```
<p>The chemist asked for a glass of H<sub>2</sub>O.</p>
```

As you would expect, user agents render sub text below other text on the same line by default, like so:

The chemist asked for a glass of H_2O.

Line Spacing, sub and sup

If you have a paragraph that has more than one line and contains one or more sub or sup elements, the spacing between the lines may vary, depending on the browser and your page's font and line-height settings. You can solve this with CSS. Solutions are available online if you search for *line spacing with sup and sub*. However, do not heed any advice suggesting you use an element other than sub or sup to circumvent this layout issue.

---

sup

A superscript

Syntax `<sup></sup>`

Attributes Core, I18n, Events, *HTML5 Only:* Global

Description

Use the sup element to mark up content suitable for superscript notation (in other words, not just because you want content to appear above the line of text).

Example:

```
<p>The mathematician wrote 4<sup>3</sup> for his age.</p>
```

As you would expect, user agents render sup text above other text on the same line by default, like so:

The mathematician wrote 4^3 for his age.

 Please see the "Line Spacing, sub and sup" box in this chapter.

tt

Teletype or monospace text

Syntax <tt></tt>

Attributes Core, I18n, Events, *HTML5 Only:* Global

Description

The tt element is purely presentational; it typically renders in the user agent's monospace font by default but conveys no meaning. tt isn't officially deprecated, but practically speaking it is, and you should not use it.

Instead, use the element that most accurately describes the meaning of the content, and then style it with CSS as desired. The code, kbd, and samp elements (all described elsewhere in this chapter) are good semantic candidates for most instances where you might have been tempted to use tt.

HTML5 and the tt Element

The tt element is obsolete in HTML5.

var

A variable

Syntax `<var></var>`

Attributes Core, I18n, Events, *HTML5 Only:* Global

Description

Use the var element to mark up a variable or computer program argument.

Examples:

```
<p>If <var>x</var> is the number of marathons Heather has
run, she has run 419.2 total miles in the races, and each
one is 26.2 miles, what is the value of <var>x</var>?</p>
```

```
<p>Einstein is best known for <var>E</var>=<var>m</var>
<var>c</var><sup>2</sup>.</p>
```

User agents typically render var in italics in the same font as other text by default, like so:

If x is the number of marathons Heather has run, she has run 419.2 total miles in the races, and each one is 26.2 miles, what is the value of x?

Einstein is best known for $E=mc^2$.

var *and the* code *Element*

There are varying opinions about whether one should use var to mark up variables inside the code element. HTML 4 isn't much help, because it simply says var "indicates an instance of a variable or program argument" and provides no examples.

General consensus is it's primarily intended for instances such as those in our examples and others representing a placeholder variable. (If you were marking up a Mad Libs sheet, you would put <var>adjective</var>, <var>verb</var>, and so on.) I suggest that if you are marking up code, var is not required, though may be used if you need to differentiate the variables from the other code (assuming you aren't emphasizing a variable, in which case em would be more appropriate).

 See the code, kbd, and samp elements for other computer- and programming-related semantics.

Embedded Content (Images and Objects)

Embedded content is typically some form of media: an image, a movie, a Flash application, and so on. In each case, it's an external resource that's loaded into your page. This chapter focuses on the elements that facilitate that.

If you're working on an HTML5 site, be sure to check out this chapter's companion, Chapter 13, which focuses on embedded content elements unique to HTML5, including audio, video, canvas, and more.

note   Looking for the embed element? Please see Chapter 13. Though in widespread use for years, it wasn't part of the X/HTML specs. However, HTML5 makes it official.

area

A region within a map

Syntax <map>
       <area> or <area />
    </map>

Attributes Core, I18n, Events, accesskey, alt, coords, href, nohref*, shape, target*, onblur, onfocus, *HTML5 Only:* Global, hreflang, media, ping, rel, type

Description

The area element defines a region within a client-side image map and may be used only in conjunction with the map element. Please see the map entry in this chapter for a full explanation.

Attributes in Detail

Please see the map entry in this chapter for more information about the alt, href, and shape attributes.

- **accesskey**: Please see "Attributes" in Chapter 1.

- **nohref**: *Obsolete in HTML5.* When present, this Boolean attribute specifies that the area doesn't have a link.

- **onblur="*script*"**: This event fires when an area loses focus, which is to say when users tab away from or click outside the defined region. It's the opposite of onfocus. As with all JavaScript events, it is best to add it unobtrusively rather than inline in the area element's HTML. (Search online for *unobtrusive JavaScript* to learn more.)

- **onfocus="*script*"**: This event fires when an *area* gains focus, which is to say when users tab to the defined region (or as they are pressing the mouse button on the link in browsers like IE and Opera). It's the opposite of onblur. As with all JavaScript events, it is best to add it unobtrusively rather than inline in the *area* element's HTML. (Search online for *unobtrusive JavaScript* to learn more.)

- **target="*frame name*"**: *Not allowed with Strict DOCTYPEs*. This defines the frame or iframe in which to open the href. Please see Chapter 10 for more details. Use it only if href is present.

HTML5 and the *area* Element

Since the nohref attribute doesn't exist in HTML5, simply don't include href to make an *area* not linked.

ATTRIBUTES IN DETAIL

Frames don't exist in HTML5, so you can use the target attribute only to point an href to an iframe.

area has these additional attributes in HTML5:

- **hreflang="*langcode*"**: This indicates the base language of the href's destination, much like the way the lang attribute specifies the language of other HTML elements. Hence, you may use hreflang only when href is present.

- **media and ping**: Please see the "HTML5 and the *a* element" box in the *a* entry of Chapter 5 for more details.

- **rel**: Please see the *a* entry of Chapter 5 for more details.

- **type="*content-type*"**: This tells the user agent the content type of the content at the link's destination. It is only advisory.

---

img

An embedded image

Syntax   `<img src="">` or `<img src="" />`

Attributes   Core, I18n, Events, `alt`, `height`, `ismap`, `longdesc*`, `name*`, `src`, `usemap`, `width`, *HTML5 Only:* Global

Description

The `img` element embeds an image in the document. Images are typically a GIF, JPEG, or PNG.

`img` use is pretty straightforward. In most cases, you'll use just the `alt`, `height`, `src`, and `width` attributes.

Example:

```
<p>
    <img src="dave_roberts_steal.jpg" width="320" height="240"
    alt="Dave Roberts slides in safely to second." />
    . . .
</p>
```

Although you can set the `width` and `height` to other values, it's best to use the image's intrinsic dimensions. If you make an image larger, it will appear distorted. If you make it smaller, you're using more bandwidth than is necessary to display the desired image size. Instead, cut out a smaller version of the image, and embed that one in your page.

The `alt` attribute is critical for accessibility, because it provides a brief description of the image as alternate text for screen readers. The text also displays in most browsers if the image fails to load or if images are turned off. If an image doesn't warrant alt text, put alt="" (screen readers typically ignore these empty alt values, but without them they'll often read aloud the img src value).

Attributes in Detail

- **alt="*text*"**: Include an alt attribute for *every* image to enhance accessibility. Please see the description just before "Attributes in Detail."

- **height="*percentage or pixels*"**: This specifies the image's height, typically in pixels. The image stretches or shrinks accordingly. When set to a percentage, it's relative to its parent container's height.

- **ismap**: When present, this Boolean attribute indicates that the image is part of a server-side image map. This type of image map is rarely used anymore, but when it is, the img must be in an a element whose href points to the server-side script. See the map entry in this chapter for an example of a client-side image map, the preferred approach.

- **longdesc="*uri*"**: *Obsolete in HTML5*. This points to a resource (that is, a text file, HTML page, and so on) with a longer description to supplement (not replace) alt when its brief description isn't sufficient. When the img is associated with an image map, describe the image map's contents.

- **name="*cdata*"**: *Deprecated in XHTML. Obsolete in HTML5*. Even though name isn't deprecated in HTML 4, always use id instead to identify an image for the purposes of scripting or styling with CSS.

- **src="*uri*"**: This specifies the image's location.

- **usemap="*#name*"**: This associates the image with a map element. It must be # followed by the map's name attribute. Please see the map entry in this chapter for an example. Note that when the usemap attribute is present, the image cannot be contained inside either an *a* or a button element.

- **width="*percentage or pixels*"**: This is the image's width, typically in pixels. When set to a percentage, it's relative to its parent container's width.

Deprecated Attributes

Use the CSS properties listed in parentheses instead of these deprecated attributes: align (float and vertical-align), border (border), hspace (margin-left and margin-right), and vspace (margin-top and margin-bottom). *All of these attributes are obsolete in HTML5.*

map

Image map container

Syntax   <map name="">
           <area> or <area />
        </map>

Attributes   Core, I18n, Events, name, *HTML5 Only:* Global

Description

An image map specifies one or more regions within a single image, typically for the purposes of linking it to another page or resource. The map element contains the *area* elements that define the linked regions.

Consider the following example, which takes a photo of items in a garage and creates links to individual pages about the washing machine, tire, and tricycle (what, you don't blog about your garage?).

Example:

```
<div><!-- it can be inside other elements, such as a p -->
    <img src="things_in_the_garage.jpg" width="400"
    height="300" alt="Things in the garage, including a
    tire, tricycle and washing machine." usemap="#garage" />
    <map name="garage">
        <area shape="rect" coords="16,21,132,152"
        href="washing-machine.html" alt="Learn about the
        washing machine" />
        <area shape="circle" coords="194,159,45"
        href="tire.html" alt="Learn about the tire" />
        <area shape="poly" coords="288,88,381,194,251,195"
        href="tricycle.html" alt="Learn about the tricycle" />
    </map>
</div>
```

The img element's usemap attribute associates the image with the map; it must be # followed by the map's name attribute. A map can be associated with more than one img in a page. (The HTML Validator may incorrectly tell you name is deprecated for Strict DOCTYPEs.)

Each area element defines a region within the image, and href defines the region's link destination URI. There are four shape values from which to choose: circle, poly, rect, and default. Declare a shape with the shape attribute, and define its coordinates with coords (they're relative to the top-left corner of the image).

Here are the rules:

- When shape="circle", the coords attribute takes three numbers: the *x, y* coordinates of the circle's center (for example, 194, 159) and the circle's radius (for example, 45).

- When shape="poly", the coords attribute takes three or more pairs of *x, y* coordinates to define a polygon. In the example, the three points are 288,88 and 381, 194 and 251, 195.

- When shape="rect", coords takes two pairs of numbers to define a rectangle. The first two represent the *x, y* coordinates of the top-left corner (for example, 16, 21), and the second two are the bottom-right corner (for example, 132, 152).

- When shape="default", it specifies the entire image (coords is not required).

- When shape isn't included, the region shape defaults to rect.

The alt attribute on area is much different than it is on an img. It should read like link text regarding the href destination (see the example), *not* describe that region of the image. alt is available to screen reader users so they'll know why to follow a link. Internet Explorer displays it as a tooltip. Use the title attribute to display a tooltip for all browsers, but always include alt regardless unless you haven't defined href.

tip In reality, most people use a tool to draw the regions and generate the map and area code rather than figuring out all the coordinates by hand. Many HTML editors have such a tool built in, but if yours doesn't, search for *image map editor* online.

note Technically, map can be associated with an object or input element, too, but you'll rarely see this in practice.

Attributes in Detail

- name="*text*": Defines the name of your image map in order to associate it with an image via the img element's usemap attribute. Please see the example.

object

A generic embedded object

Syntax `<object></object>`

Attributes Core, I18n, Events, archive*, classid*, codebase*, code-type*, data, declare*, height, name, standby*, tabindex, type, usemap, width, *HTML5 Only:* Global, form

Description

The object element adds an external resource, typically media content such as Flash applications (games, video, audio, and so on) but also images, video (QuickTime, and so on), documents (PDF, Word, and so on), and Java applets (pretty rare nowadays). object's browser support varies by the type of content, so be sure to test it accordingly. By far its most prevalent use is for loading Flash applications.

The object's inner content is fallback content for search engines and browsers that don't support what the object would otherwise load. Make sure the alternative content reflects the intended content or is a message informing users how they can access it, such as where to download a plug-in.

Example 1 shows an object that loads a SWF, along with its alternative content. *Note: This is merely to demonstrate a simple* object. *I don't recommend you use this code to embed Flash because it won't stream a movie in IE. You can use SWFObject 2, discussed in a moment, for a better approach.*

Example 1:

```
<object type="application/x-shockwave-flash"
data="how_to_change_tire.swf" width="512" height="384">
```

(continues on next page)

```
<param name="movie" value="how_to_change_tire.swf" /> <!--
↪ for IE -->
<!-- Alternative content -->
<h2>How to Change a Tire</h2>
<ol>
    <li>Remove spare tire and jack from trunk</li>
    . . . remaining steps . . .
</ol>
</object>
```

You can also nest objects. If the browser can't handle the first one, it looks to the second, and so on, down to the alternative content. The bare-bones structure (in other words, without actually specifying object data to load) looks like Example 2.

Example 2 (nested objects):

```
<object><!-- Can I load this? Yes, then load it and stop. -->
    <object><!-- No, then try this (and so on for other
    objects). -->
        <p>Alternative content</p><!-- Show only if no object
        loaded -->
    </object>
</object>
```

Probably the most ubiquitous example of nested objects is SWFObject 2, a very popular method for embedding Flash in a valid, cross-browser manner. Some browsers handle nested objects better than others (please see *http://www.alistapart.com/articles/flashembedcagematch/*), so SWFObject 2 uses IE's conditional comments to provide IE with one set of object code and other browsers with another. Please see "Step 1" at *http://code.google.com/p/swfobject/wiki/documentation* for an example.

Object vs. Embed

You might be saying to yourself, "Wait, doesn't the embed element embed applications like Flash, too?" Yes, it does, but it has never been an official part of HTML until HTML5 (see Chapter 13). Although it's now a few years old, this article summarizes the two elements nicely (not just in terms of Flash embedding), describing pros and cons for each: *http://www.alist apart.com/articles/flashembedcagematch/*. Ignore its mention of SWFFix at the end, though; SWFObject 2 has replaced that method.

Attributes in Detail

- **archive="*URIs list*"**: **Obsolete in HTML5*. This space-separated list of URIs specifies the location of one or more archives (JAR files, for example) to speed up the download of the object's resources, which may include those specified by classid and data. Relative URIs are relative to the codebase attribute if it's set.

- **classid="*URI*"**: **Obsolete in HTML5*. This specifies the location of an object's implementation. For instance, classid="clsid:D27CDB6E-AE6D-11cf-96B8-444553540000" tells Internet Explorer to load the Flash ActiveX control. classid's value may be internal, like the preceding value, or point to a location on the Web.

- **codebase**: **Obsolete in HTML5*. This sets the base path for resolving relative URIs in the classid, data, and archive values. It takes precedence over a base attribute in the document head. Omit it to use the document's base URI.

- **codetype="*content-type*"**: **Obsolete in HTML5*. This indicates the content type of the classid data so the user agent can determine whether it supports the content before downloading it. It defaults to the type value if codetype is omitted.

- **data="*URI*"**: This points to the data (resource) to be embedded in the object. For example, for a PNG, it could be data="rowboat.png".

- **declare**: *Obsolete in HTML5*. When included, this Boolean attribute specifies that the object should not be instantiated when the page loads but, instead, when another element refers to it. An object with declare must have an id so it can be referenced, and the object must appear in the source before any element that refers to it. One way to instantiate a declared object is with a link, as in `<p><a href="#idOfObject">Watch the movie.</a></p>`.

- **name="*cdata*"**: This specifies the object name when it's submitted in a form.

- **standby="*text*"**: *Obsolete in HTML5*. This specifies a message to display while the object's implementation and data are loaded.

- **tabindex**: Please see "Attributes" in Chapter 1.

- **type="*content-type*"**: This indicates the content type of the data, helping a user agent determine whether to load it (in other words, if it's supported). The HTTP content type returned by the server takes precedence.

- **usemap**: This associates a map element with the object when set to the map's name attribute value. Please see the map element in this chapter for an example of usemap with img; the same principle applies with object.

- **width="*percentage or pixels*"** and **height="*percentage or pixels*"**: These specify the object's dimensions in pixels or as a percentage of its parent element's size. Though they're technically optional, some browsers require them.

Deprecated Attributes

Use the CSS properties listed in parentheses instead of these deprecated attributes: align (float and vertical-align), border (border), hspace (margin-left and margin-right), and vspace (margin-top and margin-bottom). *All of these attributes are obsolete in HTML5.*

HTML5 and the object Element

The archive, classid, code, codebase, codetype, declare, and standby attributes are all obsolete in HTML5. For all of these, with the exception of declare and standby, you can use a param element with a name equal to the attribute name (that is, <param name="archive" value="..." />) if you need to pass that data to the embedded object. Please see param in this chapter for more information.

ATTRIBUTES IN DETAIL

HTML5 requires at least the data or type attribute to be present.

- **form="*form element ID*"**: When set to a form element's id, the form attribute associates the object with that form element.

---

param

Object resource parameter

Syntax <param name="" value="">
or <param name="" value="" />

Attributes Core, I18n, Events, name, type*, value, valuetype*, *HTML5 Only:* Global

---

Description

The param element passes a parameter name and value to the external resource loaded by an object element for it to use at runtime. Each object may have multiple params. There aren't a set of param names defined in the HTML specs; it's understood that the embedded resource will know what to do with those passed to it.

object is used to embed Flash more than any type of content. Two common params to pass a SWF are flashvars and wmode. The first passes a string of variables (each separated with &) into the movie, and the second allows you to position HTML on top of a SWF with the CSS z-index property (it may impact performance, though, so keep an eye out for that).

Example:

```
<object . . .>
   . . .
   <param name="flashvars" value="content=info.xml&amp;page=3
/>"
   <param name="wmode" value="opaque" />
   . . .
</object>
```

Please also see Example 1 in the object entry in this chapter.

Attributes in Detail

- **name="*cdata*"**: The parameter name.

- **type="*content-type*"**: *Obsolete in HTML5.* Specifies the content type of value's designated resource when valuetype="ref".

- **value="*cdata*"**: The parameter value.

- **valuetype="data|object|ref"**: *Obsolete in HTML5.* Specifies the content type of the value attribute.

- When `valuetype="data"`, which is the default, it indicates that `value`'s value is passed as a string.
- You can pass in a resource from another `object` when `valuetype="object"` and `value` is a hash name of the other `object`'s `id`. Examples are `<object id="idOfObject" data="wheelbarrow.gif" type="image/gif"></object>` and `<param name="image" valuetype="object" value="#idOfObject" />` in the second object.
- When `valuetype="ref"`, `value` must be a URI where runtime values (such as an image or a sound file) are stored.

Forms

Forms drive data gathering and searching, whether it's for Web applications, soliciting user-generated content, selling products, or conducting polls.

This chapter covers the form-related elements common to all flavors of HTML, plus includes their new attributes in HTML5, which help make the Web a richer application medium.

If you're looking for an overview of forms, the form entry provides an example of a complete form along with its behavior and a description of its components.

button

A form button

Syntax `<button></button>`

Attributes Core, I18n, Events, accesskey, disabled, name, tabindex, type, value, onblur, onfocus, *HTML5 Only:* Global, autofocus, form, formaction, formenctype, formmethod, formnovalidate, formtarget

Description

The button element can be a submit button, a reset button, or a static button. In this regard, it is the same as the input elements of type="submit" or type="image" (both of which submit a form), type="reset", and type="button" (a static button).

However, button is different in that you may place HTML (text, images, and most elements) inside it and style it with CSS. (You may style input buttons, too, but they don't accept content like button.)

Example:
```
<button type="submit" name="submitbtn"><strong>Finalize
Order</strong></button>
```

The example shows a submit button and assumes it's contained in a form element. Set type="reset" for a reset button (which restores all form controls to their initial values), and set type="button" for a static one that requires adding behavior with JavaScript. Display an image button by using either an img as the content or a CSS background-image technique.

However, button has one main gotcha: unusual Internet Explorer behavior, particularly in IE6. (Yes, although IE6 is old, it remains a requirement for many if not the majority of sites.)

IE6 and 7, as well as IE8 in compatibility mode, all don't submit a button's value; they submit its *contents*—yes, the HTML that is between <button> and </button> (technically, known as its innerText). This is particularly off-putting with a form of method="get" because that HTML ends up in your query string. Note that IE8 in standards mode correctly submits the button's value, as do all other common user agents.

IE6 exhibits a larger problem when your form has multiple buttons. It submits the name of *all* the buttons, not just the one the user selected, so you can't process the form accordingly. For example, did the user select Update Shopping Cart or Place My Order?

If your form has only one button and you're using method="post" (or if the muddied query string doesn't present problems), you're OK. Otherwise, your safest bet is using input buttons, not button elements. input with type="image" often provides plenty of creative control.

Attributes in Detail

- **accesskey** and **tabindex**: Please see the "Attributes" section of Chapter 1.

- **disabled**: Please see "Attributes in Detail" for the input element in this chapter.

- **name="*cdata*"**: This specifies the button's name for the purposes of processing the form. Please see the description for the problem in IE6.

- **onblur="*script*"** and **onfocus="*script*"**: Please see "Attributes in Detail" for the input element in this chapter.

- **type="button|reset|submit"**: Please see the description for details of the three types. If type is unspecified, most browsers default to submit, but IE6 and 7, as well as IE8 in compatibility mode, all default to button, so they won't submit the form unless the type="submit".

- **value="*cdata*"**: This sets the button's value, which is paired with its name.

fieldset

A set of related controls

Syntax `<fieldset>`

      `<legend></legend>`

      `. . . [form controls] . . .`

    `</fieldset>`

Attributes Core, I18n, Events, *HTML5 Only:* Global, `disabled`, `form`, `name`

Description

The `fieldset` element groups together one or more related form controls. The optional `legend` element identifies the group, displays in the page, and is read by screen readers. Please see the example and discussion in the `form` element entry in this chapter.

HTML5 and the `fieldset` Element

The `fieldset` element supports these additional attributes in HTML5.

ATTRIBUTES IN DETAIL

- `disabled`: Please see "Attributes in Detail" for the `input` element in this chapter.

- `form="form id"`: Please see the "HTML5 and the `input` Element" box in this chapter.

- `name="cdata"`: This specifies the `fieldset` element's name.

---

form

An interactive form

Syntax `<form action="">`
           `. . . [your form] . . .`
           `</form>`

Attributes Core, I18n, Events, accept*, accept-charset, action, enctype, method, name, onreset, onsubmit, *HTML5 Only:* Global, autocomplete, novalidate, target

Description

Use the form element and its controls to collect data from users. Uses include enabling registering on a site, submitting shipping and credit card information, conducting a poll, gathering user comments on a blog or news site, and so on. (Please note that you may not nest a form element inside another one.)

A form contains one or more controls (button, input, select, and textarea) with which the user can engage, as well as other elements (fieldset, label, and legend) that add semantic and structural meaning.

The upcoming code example results in this form default rendering:

Public Radio Station Listener Survey

Full Name: [   ]

Gender
  ○ Female   ○ Male

Country: [Afghanistan ▾]

Comments:
[   ]

☑ Yes, I'm a current subscriber

[Submit My Information]

Elements look different depending on the browser and platform. You can dictate the appearance with CSS to varying degrees.

The code that follows contains all but two of the available form child elements so you can see how they work together (button and optgroup are the only ones not shown, but they're described in their respective entries in this chapter). I've broken the code into two parts to make it easier to discuss and have highlighted at least one instance of each form-related element and attribute the example uses.

Example (part 1):

```
<h1>Public Radio Station Listener Survey</h1>
<form action="process-form.php" method="post">
   <div> <!-- text input -->
      <label for="fullname">Full Name:</label>
      <input type="text" id="fullname" name="fullname"
      maxlength="100" />
   </div>

   <fieldset> <!-- radio buttons -->
      <legend>Gender</legend>
      <input type="radio" id="female" name="gender"
      value="female" /> <label for="female">Female</label>
      <input type="radio" id="male" name="gender"
      value="male" /> <label for="male">Male</label>
   </fieldset>
   . . . [code from Example (part 2)] . . .
```

 I use a div in the example to contain most form elements. Some prefer to use a fieldset for each or lis within a list. There are no set rules about this as long as you *don't* use a table.

This part of the example includes the form, fieldset, legend, label, and text input type elements and radio button input type elements.

The form element's start tag begins each form. In the example, the action="process-form.php" value specifies the server-side location that is sent the form data for processing once the user submits it via the Submit My Information button at the end of part 2 of the example. Please see "Attributes in Detail" concerning method="post".

Each form control has a name attribute, which is paired with its value attribute. The value is typically dictated by what the user enters or selects. When a form is submitted, each control name with a value is passed to the processing script. The name must be unique throughout a form, with the exception of a related set of radio buttons or check boxes. For instance, in part 1 of the example, there's a radio button input each for female and male, but both have name="gender". Their value attributes are different, though; the form submits the value of "female" if the user selects that option and "male" for the other.

The label element's text describes a form field (for example, <label for="fullname">Full Name:</label>). Each label element is explicitly associated with a control when its for attribute value is the same as a control's id. For instance, in part 1 of example, because the first label has for="fullname", it's associated with this control: <input type="text" id="fullname" name="fullname" maxlength="100" /> (a control's name and id values are often the same but don't have to be).

> **note** Do not use a specific name (for example, name="email") on one element and the same id value (for example, id="email") on a different element, or you're bound to run into problems in Internet Explorer if you try to access the elements with JavaScript.

The fieldset element groups together one or more related form controls. The optional legend element identifies the group and displays in the page. For example, a fieldset contains our gender-related radio buttons, and <legend>Gender</legend> describes the group. legend is crucial for screen reader users because it provides context to the fieldset's controls.

That covers the highlights of the first part of our form. Now let's look at the second part. Again, I've highlighted portions that I'll discuss after the code.

Example (part 2):

```
. . . [code from Example (part 1)] . . .
   <div> <!-- select box -->
      <label for="country">Country:</label>
      <select id="country" name="country">
         <option value="AF">Afghanistan</option>
         <option value="AL">Albania</option>
         . . . [more country options] . . .
      </select>
   </div>

   <div> <!-- textarea -->
      <label for="comments">Comments:</label>
      <textarea id="comments" name="comments" rows="3"
      cols="40"></textarea>
   </div>

   <div> <!-- checkbox -->
      <input type="checkbox" id="subscribed"
      name="subscribed" checked="checked" /> <label
      for="subscribed">Yes, I'm a current subscriber</label>
   </div>

   <div> <!-- submit -->
      <input type="submit" value="Submit My Information" />
   </div>
</form>
```

Part 2 of the example includes the `select`, `option`, `textarea`, checkbox input type, and `submit` button `input` type elements.

A `select` box includes one or more `option` elements that represent the choices a user may make. For instance, in the case of `<option value="AF">Afghanistan</option>`, *Afghanistan* appears on-screen. If the user selects it, the AF value is passed to the server upon submission.

A `textarea` is different from a `text` input (see part 1 of the example) because it can be several lines tall, as defined by the `rows` attribute and because you can't set a `maxlength` in X/HTML (you can control it with JavaScript, however). The `cols` attribute specifies the number of characters allowed on a line, effectively defining its width. You'll notice different rendering sizes across browsers; use the CSS `height` and `width` properties to normalize the dimensions.

Next up is an `input` with a type of checkbox. You'll notice the `checked="checked"` attribute in part 2 of the example code. This preselects the check box. (Note: checked="checked" is the XHTML syntax; use simply checked for HTML 4, though either format is acceptable in HTML5.)

The example's `<input type="submit" value="Submit My Information" />` code displays a button that reads *Submit My Information*—or whatever you specify as the `value`. Because the `input` is set to `type="submit"`, the `form` is submitted when the user engages the button.

This should give you a sense of how a form works. Please see the other entries in this chapter for additional details about the form-related elements and their attributes.

Attributes in Detail

- **accept="*content-type list*"**: *Obsolete in HTML5*. Please see "Attributes in Detail" for the `input` element in this chapter.

- **accept-charset="*charset list*"**: This space- and/or comma-delimited list indicates the character encodings for input data that the server processing the form accepts. Typically, it's left out, since the default value is the reserved string, "UNKNOWN," which browsers may interpret as the character encoding (such as utf-8) of the page that contains the form.

- **action="*uri*"**: *Required in X/HTML*. This attribute points to the server location that will process the form when it is submitted (please see the example). If omitted, the form will submit to the current page.

- **enctype="*content-type*"**: When method="post", this attribute can be used to specify the encoding of the form data sent to the server. Typically, it's left out (the default value is application/x-www-form-urlencoded); however, you should include it as enctype="multipart/form-data" if your form includes an input with type="file". The third possible value is text/plain (data is largely unencoded when submitted), but it is used rarely.

- **method="get|post| plus delete|put for HTML5"**: The method="post" declaration means that upon submission, the form values are sent to the server without being exposed to the user. It is the more secure method. Generally speaking, it's the method of choice whenever you want to post information to the server to save, update, or remove data in a database. An example is a shipping address and credit card information form on an e-commerce site.

  When method="get", the values are appended to the action value's URI followed by a question mark. Generally speaking, use method="get" whenever you want to get information from the server after the form is submitted. An example is a search form that returns results. If action="search-results.php" and the search input text field has a name="searchphrase" attribute, then the tail end of the

URI would be *search-results.php?searchphrase=Kermit+and+Yoda* after searching for *Kermit and Yoda*.

HTML5 includes two more method values, delete and put, which map to the HTTP DELETE and HTTP PUT methods, respectively.

- **name="*cdata*"**: This attribute was included for backward compatibility with much older user agents, but you should use id instead to apply a unique identifier (for example, <form id="signup" . . .>) for styling or scripting purposes.

- **onreset="*script*"**: This event fires when the user activates an input button with type="reset". Attach this event unobtrusively instead of as an attribute in the HTML.

- **onsubmit="*script*"**: This event fires when the form is submitted, allowing you to execute JavaScript, such as a function that submits the form via Ajax instead of a page refresh in cases where scripting is enabled. Attach this event unobtrusively instead of as an attribute in the HTML.

HTML5 and the form Element

The form element has three additional attributes in HTML5.

ATTRIBUTES IN DETAIL

- **autocomplete**: Please see the "HTML5 and the input Element" box in this chapter.

- **novalidate**: When present, this Boolean attribute indicates that the form's data should not be validated when it's submitted.

- **target="*name*"**: This sets the target of the form submission and can have a value of _blank, _parent, _self, or _top, or a value you specify that could match the name of an iframe.

input

An input control

Syntax `<input type="" />` or `<input type="" />`

Attributes Core, I18n, Events, accept, accesskey, alt, checked, disabled, ismap, maxlength, name, onblur, onchange, onfocus, onselect, readonly, size, src, tabindex, type, usemap, value, *HTML5 Only:* Global, autocomplete, autofocus, disabled, form, formaction, formenctype, formmethod, formnovalidate, formtarget, height, list, max, min, multiple, pattern, placeholder, required, step, width

Description

The input element is the most diverse of the form controls, since it can be a check box, a radio button, a single-line text entry field, hidden from the user, a means to upload a file, an image button for submitting a form, and more. The type attribute dictates which of these shapes an input takes.

Examples of each type:

```
<input type="button" name="calculate" value="Calculate" />
<input type="checkbox" name="newsletter" value="technology" />
<input type="file" name="uploadedvideo" />
<input type="hidden" name="productids" value="19382, 10375" />
<input type="image" name="submit" src="btn_submit.png"
alt="Submit Form" />
<input type="password" name="password" maxlength="25" />
<input type="radio" name="color" value="blue" />
<input type="reset" name="reset" value="Reset Form" />
<input type="submit" name="submit" value="Place Order" />
<input type="text" name="firstname" maxlength="50" />
```

note   Please see the form entry in this chapter for an example regarding
inputs of type="checkbox", type="radio", type="submit", and
type="text", including a screen shot of how they render by default.

An input of type="button" renders a button that does not submit the
form when the user activates it. The value attribute provides the text that
appears on the button. You may use JavaScript to apply behavior to it.

An input of type="checkbox" is like an on/off switch. Its value is submitted only when the box is selected ("on"). Like radio buttons, a set of
related check boxes may have the same name attribute; however, in
such a case, their value attributes should be different. For instance, you
might offer several e-mail newsletters for which users can sign up. Your
check boxes could be <input type="checkbox" name="newsletter"
value="design" /> and <input type="checkbox" name="newsletter"
value="technology" />. A user may select multiple check boxes.

An input of type="file" allows users to browse on their computer or
network for a file to upload.

An input of type="hidden" doesn't display, and the user cannot change
its value. A hidden input allows you to pass data from page to page.

An input of type="image" displays a submit button that is represented
by the src attribute. When the form is submitted, the passed data is
name.x=x-value and name.y=y-value. The name is the element's name
attribute value. x-value and y-value are the x and y pixel coordinates—
measured from the top left corner of the image—of where the user
clicked within the image (if a mouse or similar pointing device was used).

Use an input of type="password" when requesting a user's password. It
renders like a text input except that for privacy, dots, or a similar character display instead of the characters the user enters.

An input of type="radio" displays a radio button. Radio buttons typically come in sets of at least two (otherwise use a check box). Unlike a
check box, a user may select only one radio button from a set of them
sharing the same name attribute. However, like with a check box, make
sure each related radio button has a different value. Please see the
gender example and description in the form entry in this chapter.

An input of type="reset" displays a button that resets all controls to
their initial values (that is, prior to user involvement). The text on the
button reads *Reset* unless you override it with the value attribute.

An input of type="submit" displays a button that submits the form
when the user activates it. The text on the button reads *Submit* unless
you override it with the value attribute.

An input of type="text" provides a single-line text box with an optional
maxlength attribute that limits the number of characters accepted by the
box. If value is set, its text appears in the text input by default. Use the
textarea element (also in this chapter) to allow for a longer, multiline
text entry.

Attributes in Detail

- **accept=*"content-type list"***: **Obsolete in HTML5*. This attribute specifies
  a comma-separated list of media types a user agent *may* use to verify
  that files submitted by a form via an input type="file" is acceptable.
  However, browser support is poor, so you shouldn't rely on it. Be sure
  your server-side form-processing script performs all required validation
  of uploaded files.

- **accesskey**: Please see the "Attributes" section of Chapter 1.

- **alt=*"text"***: This behaves like alt on the img element—providing alternate text when the image doesn't display—except in this case it's for
  an input of type="image".

- **checked**: When present, this Boolean attribute preselects inputs of type="checkbox" and type="radio". As with other Boolean attributes, it takes a different form depending on the markup language version (as specified by the DOCTYPE). checked="checked" is the XHTML syntax; use simply checked for HTML 4, though either format is acceptable in HTML5.

- **disabled**: When present, this Boolean attribute disables the element so the user can't interact with it. Furthermore, a disabled control doesn't receive focus, it is skipped in tabbing navigation, and its value is not submitted with the form.

- **ismap**: When present, this Boolean attribute specifies that an input of type="image" is a server-side image map. You'll rarely, if ever, see this used these days.

- **maxlength="*number*"**: This specifies the maximum number of characters allowed in a type="text" field.

- **name="*cdata*"**: This assigns a name to the input, which is paired with its value when processing the form.

- **onblur="*script*"** and **onfocus="*script*"**: These events are opposites. onblur fires when focus leaves the element, such as when the user tabs away from it or clicks outside it, while onfocus fires when focus is restored. As with other events, add them unobtrusively with JavaScript rather than hard-coding them in the HTML.

- **onchange="*script*"**: This event fires when the user changes the content.

- **onselect="*script*"**: This event fires when the user selects content in an input of type="text".

- **readonly**: When present, this Boolean attribute prohibits the user from altering the element's contents. The element still may receive focus, be tabbed to with the keyboard, and submits with the form.

- **size=*"number"***: This sets the number of characters that are visible for an input of type="text". Rendering varies across browsers, so use the CSS width property for finer control and more consistency.

- **src="*uri*"**: This specifies the location of the image for an input of type="image".

- **tabindex**: Please see the "Attributes" section of Chapter 1.

- **type="text|password|checkbox|radio|submit|reset|file|hidden| image|button"**: Please see the descriptions of each type in this entry.

- **usemap**: When present, this Boolean attribute specifies that an input of type="image" is a client-side image map. Please see the entry for the map element in Chapter 6 for more details.

- **value**: This is the value of the input that is associated with its name, both of which are passed to the processing script when the form is submitted.

HTML5 and the input Element

One of HTML5's primary goals is to provide native elements that enable creating Web applications more easily. In that vein, it makes big advances in the form department, especially as it pertains to input types and other attributes.

ATTRIBUTES IN DETAIL

- **autocomplete="on|off"**: Many browsers store values you've entered in a text field (with a particular name) for subsequent use when filling out another form. For instance, no doubt you've found yourself typing your city or e-mail address in a text field, only to see it appear in a small menu from which to choose. It's handy when you're using the form, but it's dangerous if someone else uses your browser later. They may be exposed to sensitive

HTML5 and the **input** Element (continued)

information (such as a credit card number) you've entered. When
you set autocomplete="off", the user agent won't do this. The
default value is that of the autocomplete setting for the input's
form owner--which is the nearest form element that contains the
input--or that is associated with the field via the input's form *attribute*. A form element's autocomplete defaults to on, so be sure to
set autocomplete="off" for all sensitive input fields.

- **autofocus**: When present, this Boolean attribute tells the browser
  to set focus on the field as soon as the page is loaded. This allows
  users to use the control without having to tab to it or click it first.

- **form="*form id*"**: By default, each form control is associated with
  its nearest ancestor form element (that is, the form that contains
  it). Set this attribute to the id of a different form in the page to
  override this behavior.

- **formaction, formenctype, formmethod, formnovalidate**, and
  formtarget: These are the same as the form element's action,
  enctype, method, novalidate, and target attributes, respectively,
  except you may assign them to a submit button. If they aren't
  present, they default to the related attribute values of the input's
  form owner (see the autocomplete attribute).

- **height="*number of pixels*"** and **width="*number of pixels*"**:
  These specify the height and width, respectively, of an input of
  type="image".

- **list="*datalist id*"**: This identifies an element that lists predefined
  options suggested to the user in a datalist element (see Chapter
  14). Its value should match the id of the relevant datalist in the
  same document.

- **max** and **min**: These indicate the range of acceptable values for
  inputs that are of type date, datetime, datetime-local, month,
  number, range, time, and week.   *(continues on next page)*

HTML5 and the `input` Element (continued)

- **`multiple`**: When present, this Boolean attribute specifies the user is allowed to enter more than one value in the `input` field. It applies only to inputs of `type="email"` and `type="file"`.

- **`pattern="`*regular expression*`"`**: This specifies a regular expression—the same kind you use in JavaScript per ECMAScript—against which the browser should check the `input`'s `value` when a `form` is submitted (but before it's sent to the server). Please see the "Patterns" section of the ECMAScript spec: *http://www.ecma-international.org/publications/files/ECMA-ST/ECMA-262.pdf*.

  For example, you would check for a five-digit numeric pattern with `<input pattern="[0-9]{5}" name="zipcode" title="A zip code requires five numbers." />`. You should include a `title` attribute that describes the required pattern; user agents display it to users as a hint. `pattern` is a welcome addition to HTML5 since it alleviates the need to write JavaScript for client-side form validation (of course, you should *always* do server-side validation regardless).

- **`placeholder="`*text*`"`**: This defines a word or brief phrase that displays in the element as a hint to what the user should enter in the field. When the user tabs to the field, clicks it, or has previously entered text in it, the `placeholder` value doesn't show. It applies only to an `input` of `type="text"` and a `textarea` element. It shouldn't be used as a replacement for the `label` element.

- **`required`**: When present, this Boolean attribute requires the user to engage the `input` (that is, make a selection or enter text, as the case may be) before submitting the form. User agents may alert users when they've failed to complete the field (try it in Opera 10.5 to see it in action!).

- **`step`**: According to HTML5, this "indicates the granularity that is expected (and required) of the control's value, by limiting the allowed values." It applies to `inputs` that are of type `date`, `datetime`, `datetime-local`, `month`, `number`, `range`, `time`, and `week`.

HTML5 and the input Element (continued)

- **type="color|date|datetime|datetime-local|email|month|number |range|search|tel|time|url|week"**: These additional input types are one of HTML5's biggest features. Where supported, validation occurs natively in the browser. The email, search, tel, and url types are specific types of text fields. The others provide new kinds of controls, such as a color picker for color and those described in "Examples of New input Types."

EXAMPLES OF NEW input TYPES

Here are a few examples of the new input types. Opera has the best support at the time of this writing. Nonsupporting browsers typically fall back to an input of type="text". Please see *http://www.htmlfiver.com/extras/inputs/* for more information about the new types (and more examples).

The date type provides a calendar. In this example, the user must select a date on or after June 11, 2010. (datetime, datetime-local, month, and week also provide a calendar, though their allowed values differ. datetime and datetime-local also show a time control like the kind type="time" displays.)

```
<input type="date" name="eventdate" min="2010-06-11" />
```

The number type shows a text field and spinner control. In this example, the user is required to select a number, and it must be between 10 and 25:

```
<input type="number" name="quantity" min="10" max="25"
required="required" />
```

The range type shows a slider control. In this example, the value is between 100 and 500 in increments of 10.:

```
<input type="range" name="pick" min="100" max="500"
step="10" />
```

label

A form control label

Syntax `<label for=""></label>`

Attributes Core, I18n, Events, accesskey, for, onblur, onfocus, *HTML5 Only:* Global, form

Description

Use the `label` element to associate a text label with a form control. Set its `for` attribute to the control's `id` to make the association; this is crucial for accessibility. Many browsers put the cursor focus inside the `input` (or select the choice in the case of a `radio` button or `checkbox`) if the user clicks the `label` text.

Example:

```
<label for="address">Street Address:</label> <input
type="text" id="address" name="address" />
```

Please also see the example and discussion in the `form` element entry in this chapter.

> **note** You are allowed to wrap `label` around controls, such as a check box input. However, some screen readers may fail to announce the control contained in the `label`, so be sure to test your form. When in doubt, stick with the model shown in the example.

Attributes in Detail

- **accesskey**: Please see the "Attributes" section of Chapter 1.

- **for="*control id*"**: Associates the `label` with a control when set to the control's `id`.

- onblur="*script*" and onfocus="*script*": These events are opposites. onblur fires when focus leaves the label, while onfocus fires when it is restored.

HTML5 and the label Element

The label element has one additional attribute in HTML5.

ATTRIBUTES IN DETAIL

- form="*form id*": Please see the "HTML5 and the input Element" box in this chapter.

---

legend

A fieldset caption

Syntax   `<fieldset>`
            `<legend></legend>`
            `. . . [form controls] . . .`
            `</fieldset>`

Attributes   Core, l18n, Events, accesskey, *HTML5 Only:* Global

Description

The optional legend element identifies the group of controls contained within a fieldset. The legend displays in the page and is read by screen readers, providing visually impaired users context for the related form controls. Please see the example and discussion in the form element entry in this chapter.

Attributes in Detail
- **accesskey**: Please see the "Attributes" section of Chapter 1.

Deprecated Attributes
The align attribute is deprecated.

optgroup

A group of select choices

Syntax   `<optgroup label="">`
              `<option></option>`

              `. . .`

              `</optgroup>`

Attributes Core, I18n, Events, disabled, label, *HTML5 Only:* Global

Description

Use the optgroup element to organize one or more groups of related option elements in a select element. Each optgroup must contain at least one option.

Example:

```
. . .
  <select name="computers">
     <optgroup label="Desktops">
        <option value="xyz2000">The XYZ 2000</option>
        . . . [more Desktop options] . . .
     </optgroup>
     <optgroup label="Laptops">
```

```
      . . . [Laptop options] . . .
    </optgroup>
  </select>
. . .
```

Typically, optgroup renders by default like this:

Attributes in Detail

- **disabled**: Please see "Attributes in Detail" for the input element in this chapter. Both Internet Explorer 6 and 7 ignore it on optgroup.

- **label="*cdata*"**: *Required.* This provides the group's label that displays in the select box above the optgroup's options.

option

A select element choice

Syntax <option></option>

Attributes Core, I18n, Events, disabled, label, selected, value, *HTML5 Only:* Global

Description

The option element provides a choice within a select element.

Please see the form and optgroup element entries in this chapter for examples and more information.

Attributes in Detail

- **disabled**: Please see "Attributes in Detail" for the input element in this chapter. Both Internet Explorer 6 and 7 ignore it on option.

- **label="*cdata*"**: If label text is specified, user agents are supposed to render it instead of the text inside the option. Only Chrome, Opera, and Safari support it among popular browsers.

- **selected**: When present, this Boolean attribute preselects the option. More than one option may be preselected if the multiple attribute is set on the select element.

- **value="*cdata*"**: This is the value submitted with the form if the user chooses the option. If the value attribute isn't specified, the option's inside text, for instance, <option>Ground Shipping</option>, is its value.

HTML5 and the option Element

HTML5's datalist element may contain one or more option elements. Please see Chapter 14 for details.

---

select

A menu of choices

Syntax <select name="">
          <option></option>
        </select>

Attributes Core, I18n, Events, disabled, name, multiple, size, *HTML5 Only:* Global, autofocus, form

Description

Use the select element to provide one or more choices in a single "menu." Each choice is represented by an option element, which may either exist on its own or exist as part of an optgroup. Please see the examples in the form and optgroup element entries in this chapter.

Attributes in Detail

- **disabled**: Please see "Attributes in Detail" for the input element in this chapter.

- **name="*cdata*"**: This specifies the select element's name so the form-processing script can associate the selected options with the select.

- **multiple**: When present, this Boolean attribute allows for more than one choice from the select box.

- **size="*number*"**: By default, a select displays only one option when the user hasn't expanded the list. Set the size attribute (for example, size="3") to the number of options you want to show instead. (Note: Chrome and Safari may show more options than desired when size is less than 5.) Typically, when size is set, a select renders as a list box with a scroll bar on the right.

HTML5 and the select Element

The select element supports the autofocus and form attributes in HTML5. Please see the "HTML5 and the input Element" box in this chapter.

textarea

Multiline field for text

Syntax `<textarea></textarea>`

Attributes Core, I18n, Events, accesskey, cols, disabled, name, onblur, onchange, onfocus, onselect, readonly, rows, tabindex, *HTML5 Only:* Global, autofocus, form, maxlength, placeholder, required, wrap

Description

A `textarea` element is a multiline text control. It is useful in cases when you would like to provide more space for content than an `input` of `type="text"` comfortably allows, for example, when soliciting reader feedback on a blog entry or a product page. You can prepopulate a `textarea` with content by placing it between `<textarea>` and `</textarea>`. Please see the example and discussion in the `form` element entry in this chapter.

Attributes in Detail

- **accesskey**: Please see the "Attributes" section of Chapter 1.

- **cols="*number*"**: *Required in X/HTML.* This sets the maximum number of characters per line, effectively setting the `textarea`'s width unless you overwrite it with the CSS `width` property.

- **disabled**: Please see "Attributes in Detail" for the `input` element in this chapter.

- **name="*cdata*"**: This specifies the `textarea`'s name for the purposes of processing the form and this element's value.

- **onblur="*script*"** and **onfocus="*script*"**: Please see "Attributes in Detail" for the `input` element in this chapter.

- **onchange="*script*"**: This event fires when the user changes the content. Since textarea doesn't have a maxlength attribute in X/HTML (it does in HTML5, although most browsers don't honor it yet), you can write JavaScript that will check for the length of the content each time it changes and prevent the user from typing more if it exceeds the limit you determine.

- **onselect="*script*"**: This event fires when the user selects content in the textarea.

- **readonly**: When present, this Boolean attributes prohibits the user from altering the textarea's contents. The element still may receive focus, be tabbed to with the keyboard, and submits with the form. One common use is on a textarea that contains terms of use copy, followed by a check box input asking the user to select it to agree to the terms.

- **rows="*number*"**: *Required in X/HTML.* This sets the number of rows of text, effectively setting the textarea's height unless you overwrite it with the CSS height property.

- **tabindex**: Please see the "Attributes" section of Chapter 1.

HTML5 and the textarea Element

The textarea element supports these additional attributes in HTML5.

ATTRIBUTES IN DETAIL

- **autofocus**: Please see the "HTML5 and the input Element" box in this chapter.

- **form="*form id*"**: Please see the "HTML5 and the input Element" box in this chapter.   *(continues on next page)*

HTML5 and the textarea Element (continued)

- maxlength="*number*": This sets the maximum number of characters allowed in the textarea.

- placeholder="*text*": Please see the "HTML5 and the input Element" box in this chapter.

- required: When present, this Boolean attribute requires the user to enter text before submitting the form.

- wrap="hard|soft": This specifies the type of text wrapping in the field. Set wrap="hard" to ensure no line has more characters than is specified by the cols attribute, which is required in this instance. If wrap is not set, it defaults to soft (the user agent figures out wrapping on its own).

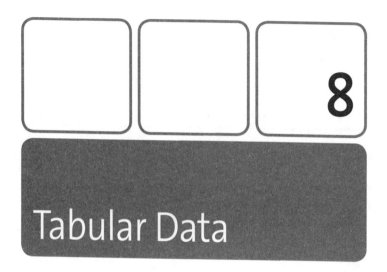

8

Tabular Data

Tabular data can take many forms such as financial or survey data, a calendar of events, a bus schedule, or a television programming schedule. Whatever the case may be, this kind of information is usually presented with one or more column or row headings along with the data.

The table element is your element of choice in these instances. It—along with its child elements—are described in this chapter. If you're looking for a code example and summary of the majority of a table's elements and features, please head to the table entry.

Note that tables are not intended to control page layout, since that's the domain of CSS (but you already knew that, right?).

caption

A table caption

Syntax `<caption></caption>`

Attributes Core, I18n, Events, *HTML5 Only:* Global

Description

The optional caption element provides a brief description of a table. It may appear directly only after the `<table>` start tag. User agents typically display the caption centered above the table by default. Please see the table entry in this chapter for an example.

Deprecated Attributes

- `align`: Use the CSS caption-side property (with a value of top or bottom) instead to dictate whether the caption should appear above or below the table. Firefox also supports additional values of left and right for caption-side, though they're no longer standard. Please note that Internet Explorer 7 and previous versions don't support caption-side. Use the CSS text-align property (with a value of left, center, or right) to control a caption's horizontal alignment.

col

A table column for styling

Syntax `<col>` or `<col />`

Attributes Core, I18n, Events, align*, char*, charoff*, span, valign*, width*, *HTML5 Only:* Global

Description

The col element allows you to apply style to one or more table columns. It doesn't impact the table's structure. All cols must go after caption or before thead if either of those elements is present. In X/HTML, they may exist on their own or be contained within one or more colgroup elements. However, if at least one colgroup is present, all cols must be in one or more colgroups. HTML5 requires all col elements to be explicitly contained inside one or more colgroups.

Please see the colgroup entry in this chapter for examples and further discussion, and see the "Attributes in Detail" section since both elements have the same attributes.

colgroup

A group of table columns

Syntax <colgroup></colgroup>

Attributes Core, I18n, Events, align*, char*, charoff*, span, valign*, width*, *HTML5 Only:* Global

Description

The colgroup element allows you to group one or more table columns for styling purposes. It doesn't impact the table's structure. colgroup may exist on its own (see Example 2) or contain one or more col elements (see Example 1), which allow more granular styling control within a colgroup. All colgroups must go after caption and before thead if either of those elements is present.

Let's add colgroup and col elements to the example from the table element entry in this chapter. I've abbreviated portions of the code surrounding the colgroups.

Example 1 (colgroup**s with** col**s):**

```
<table summary=" . . . ">
   <caption> . . . </caption>
   <colgroup class="quarter">
      <col />
   </colgroup>
   <colgroup class="years">
      <col span="3" />
   </colgroup>
   <!-- thead is here -->
   <!-- the rest of the table code -->
</table>
```

The span attribute may be used on either colgroup or col, and in either case, it indicates the number of columns the element spans for styling. (span doesn't impact the table's structure, unlike the colspan attribute that may appear on a th or td.) The class attribute (or you could use id if it's unique to the page) allows you to target CSS to a colgroup. For example, if you apply .years col { background: #ccc; width: 60px; } to the Example 1 code, each th and td in the second, third, and fourth columns will be 60 pixels wide with a gray background (the first column is dictated by the first colgroup).

There's actually more code in Example 1 than is necessary since each of the colgroups has only one col. So, you can rewrite the colgroup portion like in Example 2. In this case, the col elements are implied.

Example 2 (just colgroup**s):**

```
. . . [table start tag and caption] . . .
   <colgroup class="quarter"></colgroup>
   <colgroup class="years" span="3"></colgroup>
. . . [rest of table] . . .
```

And, in X/HTML there's yet a *third* way to write it.

Example 3 (just cols**):**

```
. . . [table start tag and caption] . . .
<col class="quarter" />
<col class="years" span="3" />
. . . [rest of table] . . .
```

In short, whether you use colgroup and/or col is up to you depending on what makes the code the lightest to accommodate your styling needs. However, you may not use a combination of Examples 2 and 3; if you use at least one colgroup, all cols must appear in one or more colgroups.

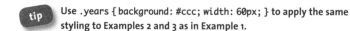

> **tip**   Use .years { background: #ccc; width: 60px; } to apply the same styling to Examples 2 and 3 as in Example 1.

> **note**   Browsers vary in what CSS styles they apply (and how you must apply them) to colgroup and col. For instance, Internet Explorer tends to support more text styling options (such as bold, italics, and alignment) via colgroup and col than other browsers.

Attributes in Detail

For align, char, charoff, and valign (all of which are obsolete in HTML5), please see "Attributes in Detail" for the tbody element in this chapter.

- **span="***number of columns***"**: Set span to the number of columns the element should represent for styling. If span is omitted, it defaults to 1. Please see the examples in this entry.

- **width="***number of pixels, a percentage value, or* 0*"**: *Obsolete in HTML5*. This attribute isn't deprecated in X/HTML, but use the CSS width property instead to set a number of pixels or a percentage (see the explanation for Example 1 in this entry). width takes a third value, too. When it is set to 0* (zero asterisk), each column should display at the minimum width necessary to contain its contents. Browser support for this value is inconsistent, though.

table

Tabular data parent element

Syntax `<table></table>`

Attributes Core, I18n, Events, border*, cellpadding*, cellspacing*, frame*, rules*, summary, width*, *HTML5 Only:* Global

Description

Use the table element to present tabular data, such as data in a spread-sheet. For instance, it could be financial or survey data, a calendar of events, or a television programming schedule. At the most fundamental level, a table is comprised of rows of cells. Each row (tr) contains heading (th) and/or data (td) cells. Several other HTML elements and attributes are particular to constructing tables, as you will see in examples here and elsewhere in this chapter.

note Although not technically illegal, do not use tables to control the layout of your pages, since it's considered a very bad and dated practice. Instead, use the proper semantics for your content and control your layout with CSS. The table element is meant to structure tabular data. (HTML e-mails are the one unfortunate exception, but that's only because not all e-mail clients and providers support, or allow, the CSS required to achieve certain layouts consistently.)

Some of the table-related elements and attributes are geared toward making a table more accessible. Sighted users may take for granted how easily they can glean information presented in a table just by glancing at it. However, imagine you are using a screen reader (or other assistive device), and the table information is read to you. It can be disorienting unless the table includes information that declares column and row headings and associates them with data cells, for instance, so the data can be announced in context.

Let's take a look at the sample table I'll explain before getting into the code. All the formatting shown is the typical default browser rendering, though as with other elements, you can style tables much differently with CSS.

I've split the table code into two parts to make it easier to discuss. I've also highlighted at least one instance of each table-related element and attribute that the example uses.

Company Financials for 1962-1964 in Thousands			
Quarter	**1962**	**1963**	**1964**
Q1	$145	$167	$161
Q2	$140	$159	$164
Q3	$153	$162	$168
Q4	$157	$160	$171
TOTAL	**$595**	**$648**	**$664**

Example (part 1—the table header and footer):

```
<table summary="Company financials from 1962-64 in which each
year is a column heading and the quarter within each year is
a row heading.">
    <caption>Company Financials for 1962-1964 in
    Thousands</caption>
    <thead> <!-- table head -->
        <tr>
            <th scope="col">Quarter</th>
            <th scope="col">1962</th>
            <th scope="col">1963</th>
            <th scope="col">1964</th>
        </tr>
    </thead>
```

(continues on next page)

```
<tfoot> <!-- table foot -->
    <tr>
        <th scope="row">TOTAL</th>
        <td>$595</td>
        <td>$648</td>
        <td>$664</td>
    </tr>
</tfoot>
<!-- Example 1 (part 2) code picks up from here -->
```

Let's discuss a few of the components shown in this first part. Not surprisingly, each table begins with the `<table>` start tag. Unlike the `summary` attribute, the optional `caption` element *does* display in the page (see "Attributes in Detail" regarding `summary`). If you include a `caption`, it must immediately follow the start tag for the `table`.

The `thead` element explicitly marks a row or rows of headings as the table head. Each row is encapsulated in a `tr` element, and each of its headings is marked up with a `th` element, as shown with `<th scope="col">Quarter</th>`, `<th scope="col">1962</th>`, and so on. `th` elements typically display in bold and center-aligned by default. The `scope` attribute does not affect presentation, but it helps make a table accessible. It informs a screen reader or other assistive device that the heading is for each `td` in a row (when `scope="row"`) or a column (when `scope="col"`) or is for a group of rows (when `scope="rowgroup"`) or a group of columns (when `scope="colgroup"`) in a more complex table.

The `tfoot` element explicitly marks a row or rows as the table foot. Sample uses include column calculations, such as in the example, or a repeat of the `thead` headings for a long table, such as a train schedule. Even though it seems counterintuitive, `tfoot` must come *before* `tbody` in the code (shown in part 2 of the example) even though it displays *after* it. (Note: HTML5 allows `tfoot` after `tbody` as long as there's only one `tfoot` in the `table`.) Please see "The `thead` and `tbody` Elements" box for more information.

> **note** You'll notice in part 1 of the example that only the first `tfoot` child element is a `th`, which is in contrast to the `thead` that has four `th`s. It's because only one of the cells is a heading, in this case for the row, as denoted with `<th scope="row">TOTAL</th>`.

All right, now onto the second part of the example, which includes the `table`'s data.

Example (part 2—the table body data):

```
. . . [tfoot] . . .
<!-- Example 1 (part 1) code precedes this -->
<tbody> <!-- table body -->
   <tr>
      <td scope="row">Q1</td>
      <td>$145</td>
      <td>$167</td>
      <td>$161</td>
   </tr>
   . . . [similarly structured tr and tds for Q2-Q4 rows]
   . . .
</tbody>
</table>
```

The `tbody` element surrounds all the data rows, which are specified by `tr` elements just like in the `thead` and `tfoot`. Each data cell is a `td`, and `tbody` is required whenever you include a `thead` or `tfoot`.

The keen observer might have spotted that the first element in the Q1 through Q4 rows is a `td` with `scope="row"`, instead of a `th`. I used `<td scope="row">Q1</td>` because each of the "Q1" through "Q4" cells in the first column is data underneath the "Quarter" column heading (<th scope="col">Quarter</th>) in the thead. When you place the scope attribute on a td, it behaves like a heading from the perspective of an assistive device. (scope on a td is obsolete in HTML5; use a th with scope instead.)

Resources to Learn More

Tables can be very complex depending on the data you need to represent. I've collected some links to resources that provide a variety of table discussions and examples, with an emphasis on making tables accessible. The links are available at *http://www.htmlfiver.com/extras/tables/*.

Attributes in Detail

- **border, frame and rules**: *All are obsolete in HTML5.* These are presentational attributes that were created before CSS had a means to provide similar control. So, although they aren't deprecated in X/HTML, use the CSS border property on the various table elements instead.

- **cellpadding="*number of pixels or percentage value*"**: *Obsolete in HTML5.* This attribute sets the amount of space around the content within each cell. Use the CSS padding property on the td and th elements instead.

- **cellspacing="*number of pixels or percentage value*"**: *Obsolete in HTML5.* This attribute sets the amount of space between each cell. There is a CSS alternative, border-spacing, but Internet Explorer 8 and older don't support it. If your goal is to remove all spacing between cells, there's a way around this; use table { border-collapse: collapse; } in your CSS instead of <table cellspacing="0"> in your HTML. However, if you'd like to set the spacing to a value other than zero (3, for example) and you want IE to display the same spacing as other browsers, you'll have to resort to <table cellspacing="3"> instead of using the CSS border-spacing property.

- **summary="*text*"**: This optional attribute provides an overview of the table structure and content to screen readers and other assistive devices. It does not typically display in the page. Reserve summary for instances when some explanatory text would be useful to the visually impaired. Please see the example in this entry.

- **width="*number of pixels or percentage value*"**: *Obsolete in HTML5.* This attribute isn't deprecated in X/HTML, but use the CSS width property to dictate the table width instead. For example, use table { width: 90%; }. When set as a percentage, the table width is relative to the width of the element in which it's contained. Browsers typically determine a table's width based on its content if width isn't specified and usually won't let it exceed the container's width (unless there's a large image in it).

Deprecated Attributes

- **align**: Use the CSS float or margin properties instead.

- **bgcolor**: Use the CSS background-color property instead.

The thead and tfoot Elements

Though not required, I recommend you include a thead in each table that has at least one row of column headings, and use tfoot as appropriate.

thead and tfoot allow browsers to differentiate a table's head and foot from its body data (in tbody) so the tbody can scroll independently of them. Also, some browsers may print the tfoot and thead elements on each page if a table spans multiple pages. Furthermore, users of assistive devices may benefit from the headings being explicitly declared, and you can gain greater CSS control.

You may nest a table inside another one, though the cases for doing so are not common. Nesting must be done within a td.

tbody

A table's body of data cells

Syntax `<tbody></tbody>`

Attributes Core, I18n, Events, align*, char*, charoff*, valign*, *HTML5 Only:* Global

Description

The tbody element contains the rows (tr elements) of data cells (td elements) that represent a table's body of data. It is required whenever a table includes a thead or tfoot element. A table may have more than one tbody. Please see the table element entry in this chapter for an example and further discussion.

Attributes in Detail

The colgroup, tbody, td, tfoot, th, thead, and tr elements share these attributes, none of which enjoys widespread use.

- **align="left|center|right|justify|char"**: *Obsolete in HTML5.* Though align isn't deprecated in X/HTML, use the CSS text-align property on tbody instead. You may also want to use the CSS margin-left:auto and/or margin-right:auto declarations on a tbody's child elements. Set align="char" when also specifying the char attribute.

- **char="*character*"**: *Obsolete in HTML5.* The intent of char is to allow you to specify a single text character that serves as the axis for horizontal alignment within cells. The default is the decimal point character for the element's language (for example, a period in English and a comma in French). However, browser support for char is virtually nonexistent.

- **charoff="*number*"**: *Obsolete in HTML5.* Used in tandem with align="char" and the char attribute, charoff is intended to allow you to specify a positive or negative numeric offset to the first occurrence of the alignment character on each line. However, browser support for charoff is virtually nonexistent.

- **valign="top|middle|bottom|baseline"**: *Obsolete in HTML5.* Though valign isn't deprecated in X/HTML, use the CSS vertical-align property on tbody instead.

td

A cell of table data

Syntax <td></td>

Attributes Core, I18n, Events, abbr*, align*, axis*, char*, charoff*, colspan, headers, rowspan, scope*, valign*, *HTML5 Only:* Global

Description

Use the td element to specify a table data cell. Typically, a td contains numeric or text data without HTML elements, but it is valid to place both inline and block-level content in a data cell.

This example shows a brief table for the purposes of demonstrating the effect of colspan and rowspan, which can also be applied to th elements. Please see the table element entry in this chapter for a longer, proper table example and further discussion.

Example (with colspan **and** rowspan**):**

```
<table border="1">
    <tbody>
        <tr>
            <td rowspan="3">1</td>
            <td colspan="2">2</td>
        </tr>
        <tr>
            <td>3</td>
            <td>4</td>
        </tr>
        <tr>
            <td>5</td>
            <td>6</td>
        </tr>
    </tbody>
</table>
```

tip I included border="1" so you could see the cell boundaries quickly without writing CSS. This approach can be handy as you're building a table. When you're done, remove the border from the HTML and set it in your CSS if desired when styling your table.

The example typically renders like this:

Attributes in Detail

For align, char, charoff, and valign (all of which are obsolete in HTML5), please see "Attributes in Detail" for the tbody element in this chapter.

- **abbr="*text*"**: *Obsolete in HTML5*. Use abbr to specify an abbreviated version of the td's content. A screen reader might read the abbr value instead of the td value.

- **axis="*cdata*"**: *Obsolete in HTML5*. Browser support for this attribute is virtually nonexistent. In theory, it allows you to specify a space-separated list of names of your choosing as a way of categorizing a cell. Please see *http://www.w3.org/TR/html4/struct/tables.html#multi-dimension* for more information.

- **colspan="*number*"**: This specifies the number of columns the cell spans across. Please see the example.

- **headers="*list of ids*"**: This attribute performs a similar task as scope—associating tds with their headings for the benefit of assistive device users—except in a more explicit manner. Suppose you have a calendar table with two headings above the same cell, such as <th id="month" colspan="7">June</th> in one row and <th id="weekday">Fri</th> in the next. You explicitly associate a cell with these by listing their IDs (separated by a space) as the headers value: <td headers="month weekday">11: Bake sale</td>. Use headers instead of scope in HTML5 pages.

- **rowspan="*number*"**: This specifies the number of rows the cell spans. Please see the example.

- **scope="col | colgroup | row | rowspan"**: *Obsolete in HTML5 on a td but valid on a th; use on a th instead*. This benefits screen readers by specifying that the element is a heading for either a row (scope="row"), a column (scope="col"), a group of rows (scope="rowgroup"), or a group of columns (scope="colgroup"). Please see an example of scope in the table entry in this chapter.

Deprecated Attributes

- **bgcolor**: Use the CSS background-color property instead.

- **height**: Use the CSS height property instead.

- **nowrap**: Use the CSS white-space: nowrap declaration instead.

- **width**: Use the CSS width property instead.

> **tip** Unlike most other user agents, Internet Explorer doesn't display the border on an empty td, even if you type a space in it, like <td> </td>. However, it will render the border if the content is a nonbreaking space entity, as in <td> </td>. IE shows a td's background color regardless of content.

tfoot

A table foot

Syntax <tfoot></tfoot>

Attributes Core, I18n, Events, align*, char*, charoff*, valign*, *HTML5 Only:* Global

Description

The tfoot element explicitly marks a row or rows (each as a tr element) as the table foot. Please see the table element entry in this chapter for an example and further discussion, including "The thead and tfoot Elements" box. Please also see "Attributes in Detail" in the tbody entry in this chapter, since the two elements have the same attributes.

th

A table column or row heading

Syntax `<th></th>`

Attributes Core, I18n, Events, `abbr*`, `align*`, `axis*`, `char*`, `charoff*`, `colspan`, `headers`, `rowspan`, `scope`, `valign*`, *HTML5 Only:* Global

Description

The `th` element specifies the heading of a `table` column or row. Please see the `table` element entry in this chapter for an example and further discussion. Please also see "Attributes in Detail" and "Deprecated Attributes" in the `td` entry in this chapter, since the two elements are the same regarding attributes with one exception: `scope` is valid on a `th` in HTML5.

thead

A table head

Syntax `<thead></thead>`

Attributes Core, I18n, Events, `align*`, `char*`, `charoff*`, `valign*`, *HTML5 Only:* Global

Description

The `thead` element explicitly marks a row or rows (each as a `tr` element) of headings as the table head. The headings provide context to the `table`'s columns of data.

Please see the `table` element entry in this chapter for an example and further discussion, including "The `thead` and `tfoot` Elements" box. Also see "Attributes in Detail" in the tbody entry in this chapter, since the two elements have the same attributes.

tr

A table row

Syntax `<tr></tr>`

Attributes Core, I18n, Events, `align*`, `char*`, `charoff*`, `valign*`, *HTML5 Only:* Global

Description

The tr element designates a table row and may contain td and/or th elements, as is appropriate. Please see the table element entry in this chapter for an example and further discussion. Please also see "Attributes in Detail" in the tbody entry in this chapter, since the two elements have the same attributes.

Deprecated Attributes

- **bgcolor**: Use the CSS `background-color` property instead.

9

Scripting

On today's Web, client-side scripting—namely, JavaScript—makes the world go 'round. Or fade in and out. Or complete your search term as you're typing it. Or drive an interactive news module. Or control a video player. Or . . . you get the idea.

Alas, showing you how to write JavaScript or any other scripting language is beyond the scope of this book, but I will show you the *easy* part, which is getting your scripts into a page.

Please also see "Attributes" in Chapter 1 for a list of the events you can apply and capture with JavaScript.

Scripting and Performance Best Practices

A full discussion of best practices pertaining to scripts and page performance is beyond the scope of this book, but I'll touch on a few points that are high impact.

First, it helps to understand how a browser handles scripts. As a page loads, the browser downloads (if it's external), parses, and executes each script in the order in which it appears in your HTML. (See the defer attribute in the script element entry for related information.) As it's processing it, the browser neither downloads nor renders any other content that appears after the script element—not even text. This is known as *blocking behavior*.

This is true for both embedded and loaded scripts, and as you can imagine, it can really impact the rendering speed of your page depending on the size of your script and/or what actions it performs.

Most browsers do this because your JavaScript may include code on which another script relies, may include code that generates content (such as with document.appendChild()), or may include code that otherwise alters your page. Browsers need to take all of that into account before finishing rendering.

So, how do you avoid this? The easiest technique to make your JavaScript nonblocking is to put all script elements at the end of your HTML, right before the </body> end tag. If you've spent even just a little time viewing source on others' sites, no doubt you've seen scripts loaded in the head element. Outside of the occasional instance where that may be necessary, it's considered a dated practice that you should avoid whenever possible.

(continues on next page)

Scripting and Performance
Best Practices (continued)

Another simple way to speed up your script loading is to combine your JavaScript into a single file (or as few as possible) and minify the code using a tool such as the following:

- Google Closure Compiler:
  http://code.google.com/closure/compiler/ (download and documentation),
  http://closure-compiler.appspot.com (online version of tool)

- YUI Compressor:
  http://developer.yahoo.com/yui/compressor/ (download and documentation),
  http://refresh-sf.com/yui/ (unofficial online version of tool)

Each will reduce your file size, but results will vary from script to script.

Those are two common and powerful methods, but they only scratch the surface of what's possible. For in-depth discussions of script-loading methods and optimization, I highly recommend *Even Faster Web Sites* (O'Reilly) by Steve Souders and his site, *http://www.stevesouders.com*.

noscript

Script alternative

Syntax `<noscript></noscript>`

Attributes Core, I18n, Events, *HTML5 Only:* Global

Description

Content contained in a `noscript` element displays only when the user agent doesn't have scripting enabled or doesn't support the type of script specified. It can contain both inline and block-level content. You may not nest a `noscript` inside another one.

Example:

```
<script src="widget.js" type="text/javascript" />
<noscript>
    <p>This content only displays if JavaScript is disabled or
    not supported by the browser.</p>
</noscript>
```

Although `noscript` is designed as a fallback to JavaScript, it's best to avoid using it whenever possible. Instead, your page's default experience (that is, without JavaScript) should make content available to all users, while browsers with JavaScript enabled display an enhanced experience. This approach is known as *progressive enhancement*.

For example, imagine you have a carousel of a dozen image thumbnails, and if you select one, the full-size version of that thumbnail displays. Say the default experience (with CSS) is that all the thumbnails display in a grid (built as an unordered list). Selecting a thumbnail reloads the page and displays the full-size image above the grid. However, if the user

agent has JavaScript enabled, the progressively enhanced version recon-
figures the thumbnail grid into a horizontal carousel that displays four
thumbnails at a time. Users can use left and right arrows to navigate
through the carousel, and if they select a thumbnail, the full-size image
displays above the carousel without a page refresh.

HTML5 and the noscript Element

HTML5 notes that noscript should be used only when you are
serving an HTML5 document, not an XHTML5 document.

It also allows for noscript in a document head, though its content
may be the link, meta, and style elements only. This is not valid
in X/HTML.

---

script

Embed or load a script

Syntax <script></script>

Attributes charset, defer, type, src, *HTML5 Only:* Global

Description

Use the script element to import or embed a client-side script in a document. Though script supports other languages, JavaScript is undeniably
the scripting language of choice. script may appear in both the head
and body elements and multiple times within a document. However, as I
note at the beginning of the chapter, it's best to combine your JavaScript
into one file and load it at the end of your page whenever possible.

You cannot place HTML elements within a script block (you can *create* **HTML with JavaScript, however).**

You can add JavaScript to your page in three ways: by putting it in an external file, by embedding the code as the contents of the script element, or by applying it inline with an event attribute. I'll cover the first two ways (the third isn't advised).

In most cases, you'll want to house a distinct piece of JavaScript in an external file both so multiple pages can load it and because it's easier to maintain your code in one file rather than in the script blocks of several HTML files. Additionally, a user agent will cache the file after it's loaded the first time, speeding up the page load of subsequent pages on the same site that use the script.

Example 1 (import external file):

```
. . .
<body>
   . . .
   <!-- Load JavaScript for product carousel -->
   <script src="js/carousel.js" type="text/javascript">
   ➡ </script>
</body>
</html>
```

Alternatively, you can embed the JavaScript in your page; however, as noted, the first approach is usually preferred.

Example 2 (embedded code):

```
. . .
<body>
   . . .
```

```
    <script type="text/javascript">
    var Foo = window.Foo || {};
    Foo.bar = {
        . . . // rest of code
    };
    </script>
</body>
</html>
```

The type attribute is required in both cases, but src applies only to the first.

As I mentioned, you can have several script elements in a page, and they can appear in both the head and the body.

Variables and functions both embedded in a document and defined in an external file can be available to each other. In other words, each script element is not mutually exclusive. For example, it's common to see a JavaScript library loaded by one script element, followed by another script element that imports or embeds code leveraging that library.

However, you may not combine an external script call and an embedded script in the *same* script element. The embedded portion is ignored. For instance, only carousel.js executes in this example:

```
<script src="js/carousel.js" type="text/javascript">
var Foo = window.Foo || {};
Foo.bar = {
    . . . // rest of code
};
</script>
```

Attributes in Detail

- **charset**: This specifies the character encoding of a script loaded via the src attribute. It does not apply to an embedded script block (such as Example 2). Please see "Character Encoding" in Chapter 1.

- **defer** (IE6–8, FF 3.1–3.6): Please see "The script Element and Performance Best Practices" box earlier in this chapter for an explanation of how user agents handle scripts by default.

  The Boolean defer attribute allows you to tell the browser that it may choose to load and execute a script after the rest of the page has been parsed and rendered. In essence, you are indicating that your JavaScript doesn't include any code that other scripts in the page depend on or that generates HTML content. If you defer a script that does either of these, your page is not likely to render properly.

  Example:

  ```
  <script type="text/javascript" src="photo-gallery.js"
  defer="defer"></script>
  ```

  Please note defer's limited browser support, listed earlier.

- **src="*uri*"**: The src value requires a valid URI that points to your external script. The external script's language must match what you specify in the type attribute. Also, if a script element has both a src attribute (like Example 1) and embedded code (like Example 2), the latter is ignored.

- **type="*content-type*"**: Use type instead of the deprecated language attribute to specify a script's MIME type. For instance, set it to text/javascript when either embedding or loading JavaScript. This attribute is required.

Deprecated Attributes

- **language="*cdata*"**: Use type instead of language.

 Please see "Scripting and Performance Best Practices" earlier in this chapter.

HTML5 and the script Element

HTML5 introduces a new attribute to script called async.

async is a Boolean attribute that instructs a script to be executed asynchronously as soon as it is available. It may be used only on a script element with a src attribute.

Example:

```
<script type="text/javascript" src="module-slider.js"
async="async"></script>
```

You may assign both async and defer for the purposes of older browsers that support defer only. However, async takes precedence if a browser supports both attributes. Please see *http://www.htmlfiver.com/html5-browser-support/* for the latest support information.

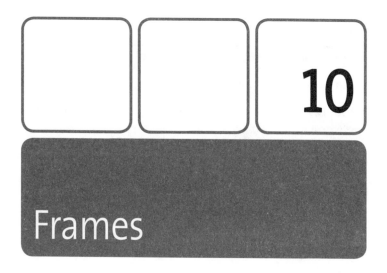

10

Frames

Frames were far more prevalent in the early days of the Web, in part because bandwidth was so poor that developers saw a benefit in splitting the screen up into pieces that loaded independently of one another. But with frames came usability, accessibility, and SEO shortcomings.

Nowadays, frames are considered a relic of the early days of the Web—so much so that HTML5 does not include them at all. Because of this, coverage here of frame, frameset, and noframes is very light.

The main focus of this chapter is the iframe element, which is very much part of HTML5, complete with some new attributes.

frame

A frame within a frameset

Syntax `<frame src="">` or `<frame src="" />`

Attributes Core, frameborder, longdesc, marginheight, marginwidth, name, noresize, scrolling, src

Description

 The frame element is obsolete in HTML5.

The frame element represents a frame within a frameset element. Please see the frameset entry in this chapter for more information.

Attributes in Detail

When present, the Boolean noresize attribute disallows the user from resizing the frame. Please see the iframe element in this chapter for details about the other attributes.

frameset

A set of frames

Syntax `<frameset></frameset>`

Attributes Core, cols, onload, onunload, rows

Description

 The frameset element is obsolete in HTML5. You can create a similar visual effect with the CSS position: fixed declaration.

The frameset element splits the window into one or more frame elements. Each frame loads its own HTML document, and navigation takes place within each frame unless a link's target attribute points to the name attribute of another frame, iframe, or window.

target also has four predefined values: _blank (opens the link in a new window; can be used in normal, nonframes pages, too), _parent (opens the link in the parent frameset), _self (the default setting; opens the link in the same frame containing the link), and _top (opens the link in the full browser window, not constrained to a frame).

Framesets may be configured in a wide variety of ways. Please see *http://www.w3.org/TR/html4/present/frames.html* for examples.

Attributes in Detail

- **cols and rows:** Each of these is a comma-separated list of the number of pixels, percentage values, and relative lengths (which use an asterisk). cols defines the layout of vertical frames, while rows defines horizontal ones. The default for each is 100%, which means one column and one row (that is, the entire screen). An example with relative lengths is cols="*, 475px, 3*". The middle column is 475 pixels wide, and the first and third columns are 25 percent and 75 percent of the remaining width space, respectively.

- **onload="*script*":** This event fires when all frame elements have loaded.

- **onunload="*script*":** This event fires when all frame elements have been removed from the window, such as when a link with target="_top" is selected.

iframe

An embedded frame

Syntax `<iframe></iframe>`

Attributes Core, `frameborder*`, `height`, `longdesc*`, `marginheight*`, `marginwidth*`, `name`, `scrolling*`, `src`, `width`, *HTML5 Only:* Global, `sandbox`, `seamless`, `srcdoc`

Description

The `iframe` element allows you to embed one HTML document inside another one. The document loaded in the `iframe` is its own entity; for example, it isn't impacted by CSS in the parent page (see HTML5's `seamless` attribute for an exception). When you activate a link in an `iframe`, it loads in the `iframe` unless it has a `target` attribute that points elsewhere. Please see the `frameset` element in this chapter for more about `target`.

Example:

```
<iframe name="embeddedpage" width="300" height="400"
src="embedded-page.html"><p>This content shows if the user's
browser doesn't support iframes.</p></iframe>
```

Attributes in Detail

- **frameborder="1|0"**: *Obsolete in HTML5*. The default value of this attribute is 1, which informs the user agent to render a border on the `iframe`. A value of 0 turns it off. Since `frameborder` is presentational in nature, use the CSS border property instead in both X/HTML and HTML5 documents.

- height="*number of pixels or a percentage value*" and width="*number of pixels or a percentage value*": This specifies the dimensions. If each is set to a percentage such as 33%, it will occupy a third of its parent element's available space.

- longdesc="*uri*": *Obsolete in HTML5.* This provides a link to a long description (to supplement the title attribute, if present) of the iframe for nonvisual user agents such as a screen reader. It is used rarely.

- marginheight="*number of pixels*" and marginwidth="*number of pixels*": *Both are obsolete in HTML5.* marginheight specifies the amount of space between the top and bottom edges of the iframe and its contents. marginwidth does the same except for the left and right sides. Although these aren't deprecated in X/HTML, they are presentational effects, so use CSS instead.

- name="*cdata*": This names the iframe so other elements may target it via their target attribute.

- scrolling="auto|no|yes": *Obsolete in HTML5.* A value of auto, which is the default state, informs the user agent to provide scrollbars when necessary. no means to never show scrollbars, and yes means always show them. Although this isn't deprecated in X/HTML, use the CSS overflow (with a value of auto, hidden, or scroll) property instead.

- src="*uri*": This is the location of the document or resource loaded into the iframe.

Deprecated Attributes

- align: Use the CSS float property instead.

HTML5 and the iframe Element

In HTML5, the iframe element does not have fallback content in between the start and end iframe tags.

HTML5 adds three attributes to iframe.

ATTRIBUTES IN DETAIL

- **sandbox**: The sandbox attribute allows you to set restrictions on an iframe's content. The value for this optional attribute is a space-separated list that includes one or more of these values: allow-same-origin, allow-top-navigation, allow-forms, and allow-scripts. When sandbox is set, the iframe's forms and scripts are disabled, its links are prevented from targeting areas outside the iframe, and its plug-ins are disabled. However, setting sandbox to allow-forms and allow-scripts reenables the appropriate elements. Scripts can never create pop-up windows, though. The allow-same-origin value treats the content of the iframe as if it were from the same origin as the parent page (that is, the page that contains the iframe). Please see *http://www.w3.org/TR/html5/text-level-semantics.html#attr-iframe-sandbox* for more details, particularly regarding warnings for certain value combinations.

- **seamless**: When present, this Boolean attribute makes the iframe's links open in the parent page instead of the iframe and makes the parent's CSS apply to the iframe's contents.

- **srcdoc**: You may assign srcdoc to a string of HTML that represents what the contents of the iframe should be. If both src and srcdoc are specified, srcdoc takes priority. This allows a legacy browser to load the src and a supporting browser to use the srcdoc value.

noframes

Frames fallback content

Syntax

Attributes Core, I18n, Events

Description

 The noframes element is obsolete in HTML5.

The noframes element provides fallback content for a user agent that doesn't support frames. Please see *http://www.w3.org/TR/html4/present/frames.html* for examples.

Part 3

HTML5 Elements and Guidance

This part of the book covers all elements that are unique to HTML5. It combines with Part 2 to detail the full set of elements available to you for HTML5 development.

Please also see "An HTML5 Overview" in Chapter 1 if you're new to HTML5.

HTML5 is still under development at the time of this writing, and although it's on stable footing, it's still subject to change. (To wit, some elements were added and removed while writing this book.) For the most part, I've left out browser support information since it often changes as vendors add more features or refine their implementations. Please see *http://www.htmlfiver.com/html5-browser-support/* for up-to-date information.

Part 3 Contents

11

Primary Structure and Sections

This chapter is a counterpart to Chapter 2 because it describes related elements unique to HTML5. If you're writing X/HTML documents, then this chapter isn't relevant. But, if you're writing HTML5, then it combines with Chapter 2 to detail all the primary structural and sectional elements at your disposal.

In X/HTML, the div element is your main device to contain chunks of content. As you know, div, although great as a container, has absolutely no semantic meaning. The seven elements in this chapter are containers that *do* have meaning. div doesn't go away in HTML5; you just won't use it as often.

Furthermore, a few of these elements directly impact a document's outline and change the way you use h1–h6 headings in HTML5. I explain that next and then get into the entries for the individual elements.

HTML5's Document Outline

Each HTML document has an underlying outline, which is like a table of contents. Now, the outline isn't something that displays in your page explicitly, but as with all semantics, it's meaningful to the likes of search engines and screen readers, which use the outline to glean the structure of your page and provide the information to users.

In X/HTML, the h1–h6 heading elements are all you have to structure the outline. HTML5, on the other hand, includes four *sectioning content* elements—article, aside, nav, and section—that demarcate distinct sections within a document and define the scope of the h1–h6 (and footer) elements within them.

This means each sectioning element has its own h1-h6 hierarchy, which is a big shift from X/HTML. Also, not only is more than h1 in a page OK, but it's recommended.

All this impacts the outline. Let's compare two equivalent outlines to see how this works. The first, which is typical in X/HTML, uses heading elements only.

Version 1:

```
<body>
    <h1>Product User Guide</h1>
    <h2>Setting it up</h2>
    <h2>Basic Features</h2>
```

```
    <h3>Video Playback</h3>
    <h2>Advanced Features</h2>
</body>
```

Now, the second version, which uses both heading and section elements, including one nested section. (Note: The code indentation is unimportant and doesn't affect the outline.)

Version 2:

```
<body>
    <h1>Product User Guide</h1>
    <section>
        <h1>Setting it up</h1>
    </section>

    <section>
        <h1>Basic Features</h1>
        <section>
            <h1>Video Playback</h1>
        </section>
    </section>

    <section>
        <h1>Advanced Features</h1>
    </section>
</body>
```

The HTML 5 Outliner (*http://gsnedders.html5.org/outliner/*) is a fantastic tool that presents a visual representation of your document's outline. Using it to generate outlines for Versions 1 and 2 shows that even though their h1–h6 heading levels are different, both result in this outline:

1. Product User Guide
    1. Setting it up
    2. Basic Features
        1. Video Playback
    3. Advanced Features

As you can see, each section element in Version 2 becomes a subsection of its nearest h1–h6 or sectioning content ancestor (also section, in this case). The same behavior is true of all four sectioning content elements (article, aside, nav, and section) even when they're mixed together.

> **note** By comparison, if Version 2 had no sections, its outline would be this:
> 1. **Product User Guide**
> 2. **Setting it up**
> 3. **Basic Features**
> 4. **Video Playback**
> 5. **Advanced Features**

Both Versions 1 and 2 are valid HTML5, but the second is preferable because the section elements are more explicit semantically. In fact, in practice I recommend you wrap an article element around Version 2's content, since that's even more appropriate in this context (though the resulting outline is slightly different). Here's an example:

```
<body>
    <article>
        <h1>Product User Guide</h1>
        <section>
            <h1>Setting it up</h1>
        </section>
        . . . [other sections] . . .
    </article>
</body>
```

Please see the section element entry in this chapter for a more complete version.

I highly recommend you create a variety of test pages and compare the results in the HTML 5 Outliner to get a better feel for how the outline algorithm works. Use the Outliner during your project work, too, to ensure your structure is as intended. First, be sure you validate your HTML5 pages at *http://html5.validator.nu/*.

This takes some getting used to for developers well versed in X/HTML but new to HTML5, because you're conditioned to think that only one **h1** is appropriate on a page except in rare circumstances. But, it makes a lot of sense if you think about it in terms of headings and sections within a normal (that is, non-HTML) document, like the kind you might write with a word processor.

Now let's dive into this chapter's elements.

article

A self-contained composition

Syntax <article></article>

Attributes *HTML5 Only*: Global

Description

The article element signifies a self-contained composition that is intended to be distributable or reusable, such as (though not necessarily) in syndication. For example, it could be a news article, a music review, a blog entry, a case study, a company's history on an About Us page, a product description, a user-submitted comment, or an interactive widget or gadget. In short, article is any independent item of content.

Naturally, a page may contain several article elements. For example, a blog's homepage typically includes a few of the most recent postings; each would be its own article.

You may nest an article inside another as long as the inner article is related to the article on the whole (please see Example 2). (Note that you may not nest an article inside an address element.)

All right, you've read about article; now let's see it.

Example 1 (basic article):

```
<article>
    <h1>The Diversity of Papua New Guinea</h1>
    <p>Papua New Guinea is home to more than 800 tribes and
    languages . . .</p>
    . . . [rest of story content] . . .

    <footer> <!-- the article's footer, not the page's -->
        <p>Leandra Allen is a freelance journalist who earned
        her degree in Anthropology from the University of
        Copenhagen./p>
        <address>
        You may reach her at <a href="mailto:leandra@
        ➥ therunningwriter.com">leandra@therunningwriter.com</
        a>.
        </address>
    </footer>
</article>
```

Note the use of the footer and address elements (see their entries in this chapter and Chapter 2, respectively). Here, address applies only to its parent article (the one shown), not to the page or any articles nested within that article, such as the reader comments in Example 2.

Example 2 demonstrates nested article elements in the form of user-submitted comments to the parent article.

Example 2 (nested articles):

```
<article>
    <h1>The Diversity of Papua New Guinea</h1>
    . . . [parent article content] . . .

    <footer>
    . . . [parent article footer] . . .
    </footer>

    <section>
        <h1>Reader Comments</h1>
        <article>
            <footer>bloose wrote on <time datetime="2010-08-20"
            pubdate>August 20, 2010</time>:</footer>
            <p>Great article! I've always been curious about
            Papua New Guinea.</p>
        </article>

        <article>
            . . . [next reader comment] . . .
        </article>
    </section>
</article>
```

 Please see the other elements in this chapter for additional examples that include article.

aside

Tangential content

Syntax `<aside></aside>`

Attributes *HTML5 Only*: Global

Description

The `aside` element indicates a section of content that is tangentially
related to the main content on the page but that could stand on its
own. It may be a box within the main content itself, in the same column
but not nested in the main content, or in (or as) a secondary column.
Examples include a pull quote, a sidebar, a box of links to related articles
on a news site or other blog entries, advertising, groups of nav elements,
and a list of related products on a commerce site.

Example 1 shows an `aside` used for an inset sidebar.

Example 1 (nested in main content):

```
<article>
   <h1>The Diversity of Papua New Guinea </h1>
   . . . [article content] . . .
   <aside>
      <h1>Papua New Guinea Quick Facts</h1>
      <ul>
         <li>The country has 38 of the 43 known birds of
         paradise.</li>
         <li>Though quite tropical in some regions, others
         occasionally experience snowfall.</li>

         . . .

   </aside>
```

```
. . . [more article content] . . .
</article>
```

That same article might include a "Related Stories" aside containing a list of links to other essays about the country or surrounding region (Indonesia, Australia, and so on). Alternatively, that aside could be in a different page column instead of nested in the article.

Now, let's consider an example of a design portfolio or case studies, in which each page focuses on a single project and you provide links to the other ones in an adjacent column (as controlled by CSS, not simply by virtue of arranging the code as shown in Example 2).

Example 2 (not nested in main content):

```
<article> <!-- main content on the page -->
    <h1>. . . [name of project] . . .</h1>
    <figure>. . . [project photo] . . .</figure>
    <p>. . . [project write-up] . . .</p>
</article>

<!-- this aside is not nested in the article -->
<aside>
<h1>Other Projects</h1>
    <nav>
        <ul>
            <li><a href="habitat-for-humanity.html">Habitat for
            Humanity brochure</a></li>
            <li><a href="royal-philharmonic.html">Royal
            Philharmonic Orchestra site</a></li>

            . . .

        </ul>
    </nav>
</aside>
```

It would be perfectly fine to nest this particular aside in the project article, too, since they are related.

On that subject, an aside nested in the page's main content typically requires a closer relationship than when it's outside. For example, if the main content is a blog entry article element, you could mark up your blogroll in a non-nested aside. It would be inappropriate to nest it in the article, because it isn't related to that specific entry—unless, of course, your blog post is "My Favorite Blogs"! Note that one other place you may not nest an aside is inside an address element.

> **note** Use the figure element, not aside, to mark up figures that are part of an article, such as a chart or graph. Please see Chapter 12 for more information.

footer

Footer of segment or page

Syntax <footer></footer>

Attributes *HTML5 Only:* Global

Description

Use the footer element to represent a footer for the nearest article, aside, blockquote, body, details, fieldset, figure, nav, section, or td element in which it is nested. It signifies the footer for the whole page only when its nearest ancestor among these is the body (see Example 1). And if a footer wraps *all* the content in its section (such as an article, for example), it represents the likes of an appendix, index, long colophon, or long license agreement, depending on its content.

A footer typically includes information about its section, such as links to related documents (see Example 1), copyright information (see Example 1), its author (see Example 2), and similar items. A footer does not need to be at the end of its containing element, though usually it is. Also, you may not nest a header element or another footer within a footer, nor may you nest a footer within a header or address element.

Even if you've never written a line of HTML5, you're no doubt familiar with the notion of a page footer. That's one such use for the footer element, as shown in Example 1.

> **tip**   Please see the entry for the header element in this chapter for an example of how the page header and content area could be structured.

Example 1 (as page footer):

```
<body>
    . . . [page header and content] . . .

    <!-- this is a page footer because body is its nearest
    ancestor -->
    <footer>
        <p><small>&copy; Copyright 2011 The Corporation, Inc.</
        ➥ small></p>

    <ul>
        <li><a href="terms-of-use.html">Terms of Use</a></li>
        <li><a href="privacy-policy.html">Privacy Policy</a>
        ➥ </li>
    </ul>
    </footer>
</body>
```

Please see the nav element entry in this chapter for an explanation of why the links ul isn't wrapped in a nav.

The following borrows from Example 1 in the article element entry in this chapter. It demonstrates a footer in the context of a page section. Please see that entry for an explanation of the address element's scope here.

Example 2 (as a page section footer):

```
<body>
    . . .
    <article>
        <h1>. . . [article header] . . .</h1>
        <p>. . . [article content] . . .</p>
        <footer> <!-- the article footer -->
            <p>Leandra Allen is a freelance journalist who
            earned her degree in Anthropology from the
            University of Copenhagen.</p>
            <address>
            You may reach her at <a href="mailto:leandra@the
            ➥ runningwriter.com">leandra@therunningwriter.com
            ➥ </a>.
            </address>
        </footer>
    </article>
    <footer id="footer"> <!-- the page footer -->
        . . . [copyright, terms of use, privacy policy] . . .
    </footer>
</body>
```

The id="footer" (call it anything you like) on the page footer is optional and is just to differentiate it from the other footer for styling control.

header

Grouped introductory content

Syntax <header></header>

Attributes *HTML5 Only*: Global

Description

Use the header element to mark up a group of introductory or navigational content. It usually includes the section's heading (an h1–h6 or
hgroup), but this isn't mandatory. Some other header uses include representing the header for the whole page or containing a search form, relevant logos, or a section's table of contents (see Example 2). See Example 1
regarding the first three. You may not nest a footer or another header
within a header, nor may you nest a header within a footer or address
element.

note Don't use header unnecessarily. If all you have is an h1–h6 or an
hgroup and no companion content worthy of grouping with it, there's
no need to wrap it in a header in most cases.

When you think of a header, no doubt a page's masthead comes to mind,
as in this common structure in X/HTML pages:

```
<body>
    <div id="header">
        . . . [site logo, global navigation, etc.] . . .
    </div>

    . . . [page content and footer] . . .
</body>
```

HTML5's header element is the right choice for replacing that div, but a header may also appear elsewhere in your pages, as shown in Example 2. But, first, let's replace that page header div.

Example 1 (as page header):

```
<body>
    <header><!-- add an id like "header" or "masthead" if
    desired -->
        <!-- site logo could go here -->
        <!-- a search box form could go here -->

        <!-- site's global navigation -->
        <nav>
            <ul> . . . </ul>
        </nav>
    </header>
    <article>
        . . . [page content] . . .
    </article>
    <footer>
        . . . [copyright, terms of use, privacy policy, etc.]
        . . .
    </footer>
</body>
```

> **tip**   Please see the entry for the footer element in this chapter for an example of how to structure a page footer.

As I mentioned, header isn't limited to containing your page's masthead. In Example 2 I've added a header that wraps both the heading and question links at the top of a FAQ. The common theme of the examples is that the header contains a group of introductory content or navigation that leads into the next section.

Example 2 (in page content):

```
<body>
    <header>
        . . . [site logo, navigation, etc.] . . .
    </header>
    <article>
        <header>
            <h1>Frequently Asked Questions</h1>
            <nav>
                <ul>
                    <li><a href="#answer1">What is your return
                    policy?</a></li>
                    <li><a href="#answer2">How do I find a
                    location?</a></li>
            . . .
                </ul>
            </nav>
        </header>

        <!-- the header links point to these -->
        <article id="answer1">
            <h1>What is your return policy?</h1>
            <p> . . . [answer] . . . </p>
        </article>

        <article id="answer2">
            <h1>How do I find a location?</h1>
            <p> . . . [answer] . . . </p>
        </article>
```
(continues on next page)

```
        . . .
    </article> <!-- end parent article -->

    . . .
</body>
```

 tip The nav element is appropriate around the list of FAQ question links since it's a major navigation group within the page, as discussed in the nav entry in this chapter.

hgroup

Group of multiple headings

Syntax <hgroup>[two or more headings]</hgroup>

Attributes *HTML5 Only*: Global

Description

The hgroup element represents a section header and may contain only two or more h1–h6 headings. It's for times when your heading has multiple levels, such as subheadings, alternative titles, or tag lines, or if you don't want those subheadings or alternate title to affect the document outline. Grouping them in an hgroup indicates they are related.

For instance, consider the news story shown in the example.

Example:

```
<article>
    <hgroup>
        <h1>Giraffe Escapes from Zoo</h1>
        <h2>Animals Worldwide Rejoice</h2>
```

```
    </hgroup>
    <p>. . . [article content] . . .</p>
</article>
```

Only the first instance of the highest-ranked heading in an hgroup appears in the document outline—"Giraffe Escapes from Zoo" in the example. Similarly, if another h1 appeared after it, it would be omitted from the outline just like the h2. Please see "HTML5's Document Outline" earlier in this chapter.

nav

Section of major navigation

Syntax <nav></nav>

Attributes *HTML5 Only*: Global

Description

X/HTML doesn't have an element that explicitly represents a section of major navigation links, but HTML5 does: the nav element. Links in a nav may point either within the page, to other resources, or both. However, use it only for your document's most important groups of links, not all of them.

nav doesn't replace the need to structure your links in an ul and ol element, as appropriate. Continue to use those elements, and simply wrap a nav around them.

HTML5 recommends not wrapping ancillary page footer links like "Terms of Use" and "Privacy Policy" in a nav, which makes sense. Sometimes, though, your page footer reiterates the top-level global navigation or includes other important links like "Store Locator." In most cases, I recommend putting those types of footer links in a nav.

The following sample news page includes four lists of links, only two of which are considered major enough to warrant being wrapped in a nav:

Example:

```
<body>
   <header>
      <!-- site logo could go here -->
      <!-- site global navigation -->
      <nav>
         <ul> . . . </ul>
      </nav>
   </header>

   <div id="main">
      <h1>Arts &amp; Entertainment</h1>
      <article>
         <h1>Gallery Opening Features the Inspired,
         Inspiring</h1>
         <p>. . . [story content] . . . </p>

         <aside>
            <h1>Other Stories</h1>
            <!-- not wrapped in nav -->
            <ul> . . . [story links] . . . </ul>
         </aside>
      </article>
   </div>

   <aside id="sidebar">
      <nav><!-- secondary navigation -->
```

```
        <ul>
            <li><a href="/arts/movies/">Movies</a></li>
            <li><a href="/arts/music/">Music</a></li>

            . . .

        </ul>
    </nav>
</aside>

<footer>
    <!-- Ancillary links not wrapped in nav. See
    Example 1 of footer entry in this chapter. -->
    <ul> . . .</ul>
</footer>
</body>
```

The secondary navigation in the aside allows the user to navigate to other pages in the Arts & Entertainment directory, so it constitutes a major navigational section.

Note that you shouldn't nest a nav within an address element.

tip   **Example 2 in the header element entry in this chapter includes an example of a nav surrounding a group of links that point within the page.**

So, how do you decide when a group of links deserves a nav? Ultimately, it's a judgment call based on your content organization and accessibility. Although this feature didn't exist at the time of this writing, a user agent such as a screen reader may choose to prioritize links contained in a nav over others. For instance, it could allow users to jump easily from one nav block to another with a keyboard command. Or a user agent may present the nav elements and suppress other links initially to assist certain users (note: this *isn't* default browser behavior).

section

Thematic content grouping

Syntax `<section></section>`

Attributes *HTML5 Only*: Global

Description

The `section` element indicates a thematic grouping of content, typically with a heading. Examples include composition sections (and subsections, if nested; see the example), chapters, or each tab within a tabbed module.

note Keep in mind that `section` is not a generic container like `div`, because `section` conveys meaning. Generally speaking, use `section` instead of `div` if its content should appear in the page's outline (see "HTML5's Document Outline" earlier in this chapter).

The distinction between `article` and `section` is a little subtle. HTML5 recommends using `article` instead if the content could be syndicated. Please see the examples throughout this chapter to get a sense of how to use `article`.

The following example, like Example 2 in this chapter's `article` element entry, shows `article` and `section` working together.

Example:

```
<article>
    <h1>Product User Guide</h1>
    . . . [introductory content] . . .

    <section>
        <h1>Setting it up</h1>
```

```
      . . . [instructions] . . .
   </section>

   <section> <!-- this contains two subsections -->
      <h1>Basic Features</h1>
      <section> <!-- nested, so it's a subsection -->
         <h1>Video Playback</h1>
         . . . [instructions] . . .
      </section>
      <section> <!-- another subsection -->
         <h1>Jumping to Chapters</h1>
         . . . [instructions] . . .
      </section>
   </section>
   . . .
</article>
```

Note that you shouldn't nest a section within an address element.

12

Text

This chapter features text-level semantics that are unique to HTML5.

Of these, you will probably find yourself using the new figure and figcaption the most, since they address a common content convention (a figure with a caption, surprise!) for which X/HTML lacks dedicated elements.

This chapter's counterpart is Chapter 5; together they detail all the text-level elements available to you when developing HTML5 documents and applications.

figcaption

Caption for a figure

Syntax `<figure>`
       `<figcaption></figcaption>`
    `</figure>`

Attributes *HTML5 Only*: Global

Description

The `figcaption` element represents the caption or legend for a `figure` element's contents. It might be a brief photo description or references that begin with "Exhibit D" and the like. You cannot use `figcaption` unless it's in a `figure` element and `figure` has other content. And although `figcaption` is optional, a `figure` may include only one, and it must be either the first or last child element of the `figure`.

Please see the `figure` element in this chapter for more details and code examples.

figure

A figure

Syntax `<figure></figure>`

Attributes *HTML5 Only*: Global

Description

Use the `figure` element to mark up a self-contained piece of content (with an optional caption) that is referred to by the main content of your document. Typically, `figure` is part of the content that refers to it, but the `figure` could also live elsewhere on the page or on another page, such as in an appendix.

A `figure` element may include a chart, a graph, a photo, an illustration, a code segment, and so on. Think of how you see figures in magazine or newspaper articles, stories, and reports, and you'll have a good sense of when to use `figure`.

The optional `figcaption` is a `figure`'s caption or legend and may appear either at the beginning or at the end of a `figure`'s content. (See the `figcaption` entry in this chapter for more details.)

Consider Example 1, an excerpt from an annual report, which includes a pie chart to supplement the primary content.

Example 1:

```
<article>
    <h1>2011 Revenue by Industry</h1>
    . . . [report content] . . .

    <figure>
        <figcaption>Figure 3: 2011 Revenue by Industry
        ➥ </figcaption>
        <img src="chart_revenue.png" width="260" height="260"
        alt="Revenue chart: Clothing 42%, Toys 36%,
        Food 22%" />
    </figure>

    <p>As Figure 3 illustrates, . . . </p>

    . . . [more report content] . . .
</article>
```

tip Note the use of the image's `alt` attribute in Example 1 to convey the chart's contents to screen readers or in the event a browser's images are turned off.

Another part of the report could include a letter from the president of a board of trustees, accompanied by her photo and a caption.

Example 2:

```
<article>
   . . .
   <figure>
      <img src="photo_president.jpg" width="200" height="300"
      alt="Gwen Chapman" />
      <figcaption>Gwen Chapman, President of the Board
      ➥</figcaption>
   </figure>
   . . .
</article>
```

Or, instead of a photo, it could be a video introduction (please see the `video` element in Chapter 13). `figure` may also include multiple pieces of content. For instance, Example 1 could include two charts: one for revenue and another for profits. Keep in mind, though, that when using a `figure` with multiple pieces of content, only one `figcaption` element is permitted.

note Don't use `figure` simply as a means to embed all instances of self-contained content within a body of text. Oftentimes, the `aside` element may be appropriate instead. Please see its entry in Chapter 11.

mark

Highlighted text

Syntax `<mark></mark>`

Attributes *HTML5 Only:* Global

Description

The mark element is like a semantic version of a highlighter pen. In other words, you don't use a highlighter because you want to color snippets of your textbook or legal document yellow; you use it because the text you highlight is especially relevant to the task at hand (such as when studying for an exam, reviewing a contract for key language, and so on). The same is true when you use mark; style its text with CSS as you please (or not at all, as is the default user agent behavior), but use it only when it's pertinent to do so.

No matter when you use mark, it's to draw the reader's attention to a particular text segment. Here are some use cases for it:

- Highlighting part of a quote that wasn't highlighted in its original form by the author to call attention to it (see Example 1).

- Highlighting a search term when it appears in a results page or an article. Suppose you searched for *megapixel* and each resulting article used `<mark>megapixel</mark>` to highlight the term throughout its text for your benefit.

- Highlighting a code fragment (see Example 2).

Example 1:

```
<p>So, I went back and read the instructions myself to see
what I'd done wrong. They said:</p>

<blockquote>
   <p>Remove the tray from the box. Pierce the overwrap
   several times with a fork and cook on High for <mark>15
   minutes</mark>, rotating it half way through.</p>
</blockquote>

<p>I thought she'd told me <em>fifty</em>. No wonder it
exploded in my microwave.</p>
```

 mark is not the same as either em (represents emphasis) or strong (represents importance). Please see their entries in Chapter 5.

Example 2 features a highlighted piece of code. (Again, the mark code won't look different unless you style it with CSS.)

Example 2:

```
<p>Experienced developers know it's bad practice to use a
class name that describes how it should look, such as with
the highlighted portion below:
<pre>
   <code>
      <mark>.redText</mark> {
          color: #c00;
      }
   </code>
</pre>
```

meter

A scalar measurement

Syntax `<meter value=""></meter>`

Attributes *HTML5 Only:* Global, `form`, `high`, `low`, `min`, `max`, `optimum`, `value`

Description

The `meter` element signifies a measurement within a known range or a fractional value. In plain English, it's the type of gauge you use to represent the likes of voting results (for example, "30% Smith, 37% Garcia, 33% Clark"), the number of tickets sold (for example, "811 out of 850"), numerical test grades, and disk usage. You may use `meter` within most other elements, though not within another `meter`.

Although it's not required, as a best practice you should include text inside `meter` that reflects the current measurement so older user agents may present it.

Examples:

```
<p>Project completion status: <meter value="0.80">80%
completed</meter></p>

<p>Car brake pad wear: <meter low="0.25" high="0.75"
optimum="0" value="0.21">21% worn</meter></p>
```

`meter` is *not* for marking up general measurements such as height, weight, distance, or circumference that have no known range. For example, you cannot do this: `<p>I walked <meter value="3">3</meter> miles yesterday.</p>`. However, you can do the following:

Example (with title):

```
<p>Miles walked during half-marathon: <meter min="0"
max="13.1" value="2.5" title="Miles">2.5</meter></p>
```

meter doesn't have defined units of measure, but you can use the title attribute to specify text of your choosing, as in the previous example. User agents might display the title as a tooltip or otherwise leverage it when rendering the meter.

note HTML5 suggests user agents might render a meter like a horizontal bar with the measured value colored differently than the maximum value (unless they're the same, of course). Think of a thermometer on its side. No browsers support this at the time of this writing. In the meantime, you can style meter to some extent with CSS or enhance it further with JavaScript.

Attributes in Detail

Each of these attributes is optional except value. And all those indicating an attribute value of *number* should be set to a valid floating-point number. Negative numbers are allowed.

- form="*form element ID*": Associates the meter with the form element whose id equals the value of this attribute. This overrides the default behavior, which is if meter is nested inside a form element, it's associated with that element.

- high="*number*", low="*number*", optimum="*number*": Work together to split the range into low, medium, and high segments. optimum indicates the optimum position within the range, such as "o brake pad wear" in one of the examples. Set optimum lower than low to indicate that low values are better, do the opposite for high, and set it in between if neither a low value nor a high value is optimal.

- **min="*number*"**: Specifies the lower bound of the range. It equals 0 if it's unspecified.

- **max="*number*"**: Specifies the upper bound of the range. It equals 1.0 if it's unspecified.

- **value="*number*"**: *Required*. Specifies the value for the meter to indicate as the value measurement. If it's less than the min value, user agents treat it the same as min, and if it's more than max, it is treated the same as max.

Furthermore, the following must be true when you apply these attribute values (LTE means "is less than or equal to"):

- min LTE value LTE max.

- min LTE low LTE max (if low is specified).

- min LTE high LTE max (if high is specified).

- min LTE optimum LTE max (if optimum is specified).

- low LTE high (if both low and high are specified).

And if a minimum or maximum isn't specified, then the value attribute must be between the range of 0 and 1.

> **note** Use the progress element (see its entry in this chapter) instead of meter to indicate a task's progress, such as with a progress bar.

progress

Task progress indicator

Syntax `<progress></progress>`

Attributes *HTML5 Only:* Global, form, max, value

Description

Use the progress element to display the completion progress of a task (like a progress bar).

For instance, a Web application could indicate the progress as it's saving a large amount of data. Although it's not required, as a best practice you should include text (for example, "0% saved," as shown in the example) inside progress that reflects the current value and max for older user agents.

Example:

```
<p>Please wait as we save your data. Current progress:
<progress id="progressBar" max="100">0% saved</progress></p>
```

Though a full discussion is beyond the scope of this book, typically you would update both the progress value and the inner text (for example, make it "20% saved," and so on) dynamically with JavaScript. var bar = document.getElementById('progressBar'); gives you access to the element from the example, and then you can get or set bar.value.

Attributes in Detail

Those indicating an attribute value of *number* should be set to a valid floating-point number.

- **form="*form element ID*"**: Associates the progress with the form element whose id equals the value of this attribute. This overrides the default behavior, which is if progress is nested inside a form element, it's associated with that element.

- **max="*number*"**: Specifies the number the value attribute must reach to signal the task is complete. It must be greater than 0, and if it's unspecified, it equals 1.0.

- **value="*number*"**: Specifies the current progress as a number. It is optional, but if it's specified, it must be equal to or greater than 0 and less than or equal to the max attribute.

note You may not nest one progress inside another one.

note There are two types of progress elements: determinate and indeterminate. A *determinate* progress has a value, so its progress can be determined by the relation of the value to the max attribute. An *indeterminate* progress does not have a specified value, so although progress may be occurring, its level can't be determined (the task may be waiting for feedback).

HTML5 suggests user agents display determinate and indeterminate progress elements differently but is short on specifics other than to say that determinate ones should show the value of value relative to the value of max. No browsers support this at the time of this writing. In the meantime, you can style progress to some extent with CSS or enhance it further with JavaScript.

rp

For ruby fallback parentheses

Syntax `<rp>(</rp>` and `<rp>)</rp>`

Attributes *HTML5 Only:* Global

Description

Use the rp element to display parentheses around ruby text (the rt element) in user agents that don't support ruby annotations. User agents that *do* support ruby ignore the rp, so they don't display the parentheses.

Please see the ruby element in this chapter for an example.

rt

Ruby text component

Syntax `<ruby>`
       `<rt></rt>`
    `</ruby>`

Attributes *HTML5 Only:* Global

Description

The rt element contains the ruby text used in a ruby annotation. The content of an rt represents the annotation of the ruby element content that immediately precedes it (not including an rp element).

Please see the ruby element in this chapter for an example.

ruby

A ruby annotation

Syntax `<ruby>`
         `<rp>(</rp><rt></rt><rp>)</rp>`
      `</ruby>`

Attributes *HTML5 Only:* Global

Description

A *ruby annotation* is a convention in East Asian languages, such as Chinese and Japanese, typically used to show the pronunciation of lesser-known characters. These small annotative characters appear either above or to the right of the characters they annotate. They are often called simply *ruby* or *rubi*, and the Japanese ruby characters are known as *furigana*.

The ruby element, as well as its rt and rp child elements, is HTML5's mechanism for adding them to your content. rt specifies the ruby characters that annotate the base characters. The optional rp allows you to display parentheses around the ruby text in user agents that don't support ruby. This example demonstrates this structure with English placeholder copy. The area for ruby text is highlighted.

Example:

```
<ruby>
    base <rp>(</rp><rt>ruby chars</rt><rp>)</rp>
    base <rp>(</rp><rt>ruby chars</rt><rp>)</rp>
</ruby>
```

A user agent that supports ruby may display it like this (or on the side):

ruby chars ruby chars
base base

If the example included the base Chinese characters for *Beijing* (which requires two characters) and their accompanying ruby characters, a user agent that supports ruby may display it like this (or on the side):

ㄅㄟ ㄐ一ㄥ
北 京

As you can see, it ignores the rp parentheses and just presents the rt content. However, a user agent that *doesn't* support ruby displays it like this:

北(ㄅㄟˇ)京(ㄐ一ㄥ)

You can see how important the parentheses are; without them, the base and ruby text would run together, clouding the message.

 note At the time of this writing, only Internet Explorer and Google Chrome support ruby annotations (all the more reason to use rp in your markup). The HTML Ruby Firefox add-on (*https://addons.mozilla.org/en-US/firefox/addon/6812*) provides support in the meantime.

tip You may learn more about ruby characters at *http://en.wikipedia.org/wiki/Ruby_character*.

time

Date and/or time

Syntax `<time></time>`

Attributes *HTML5 Only:* Global, `datetime`, `pubdate`

Description

Use the `time` element to represent a precise time or Gregorian calendar date. The time is based on a 24-hour clock with an optional time-zone offset. You may not nest a `time` element inside another one.

The `datetime` attribute provides the date and/or time in a machine-readable format. This sample demonstrates the `datetime` format:

`2011-03-25T17:19:10-02:00`

This means "March 25, 2011, at 10 seconds after 5:19 p.m." T separates the date (YYYY-MM-DD) and time (hh:mm:ss), and the time-zone offset is preceded by - (minus) or + (plus). You aren't required to provide `datetime`, and if you do, it doesn't need to be the full complement of information (see Example 1).

The optional text content inside `time` (that is, `<time>text</time>`) appears on the screen as a human-readable version of the `datetime` value.

The following examples demonstrate various `time` configurations.

Example 1 (variations):

```
<p>The volunteers arrive at <time>03:30</time>.</p>
<p>We began our hike through Zion National Park on <time
datetime="2003-07-03T10:30:00">July 3, 2003 at 10:30 am
↪</time>.</p>
<p>They made their dinner reservation for <time datetime=
↪"2010-11-02T19:15:00">tonight at 7:15</time>.</p>
<p>The record release party is on <time datetime="2010-11-02">
↪</time>.</p>
```

You'll notice that the last one doesn't have any text content. In such cases, user agents are supposed to render the datetime value as text in a human-friendly manner, but as of this writing, none yet do so. You'll have to wait until a few browsers support this rendering feature of time to see the exact results.

Use the pubdate attribute to indicate that time represents a publishing date (see "Attributes in Detail" for more specifics.)

Example 2 (with pubdate):

```
<article>
    <header>
        <h1>Popularity of Mountain Hiking Sees Steady
        Increase</h1>
        <p><time datetime="2006-06-15" pubdate>June 15, 2006
        ↪</time></p>
    </header>

    . . . [article content] . . .
</article>
```

If the article had reader-submitted comments, those could be time-stamped with `time`, `datetime`, and `pubdate`, too.

Attributes in Detail

- **datetime**: This provides the date or time being specified. If you don't include it, the date or time is represented by the `time` element's text content. Its machine-readable format (described earlier in this entry) allows for syncing dates and times between Web applications.

- **pubdate**: This Boolean attribute specifies that the `time` element represents the publication date and time of the nearest `article` element that contains the `time` element. If there isn't an `article` ancestor, the publication date applies to the whole page. If `pubdate` is included, either `datetime` or the `time` element's text content as a valid date string (such as "June 15, 2006" in Example 2) with an optional time is required. `pubdate` may be specified as either `pubdate` or `pubdate="pubdate"`. The latter is required for XHTML5.

note Do not use `time` to mark up imprecise dates or times, such as "the mid-1900s," "just after midnight," "the latter part of the Renaissance," or "early last week."

note Because dates in the `time` element are based on the Gregorian calendar, HTML5 recommends you don't use it for pre-Gregorian dates. There has been a lot of discussion about this limitation, but it's a complicated issue. Read *http://www.quirksmode.org/blog/archives/2009/04/making_time_saf.html* for an extensive explanation of some of the issues.

wbr

A line break opportunity

Syntax   <wbr> or <wbr />

Attributes   *HTML5 Only:* Global

Description

Browsers wrap text content automatically, but sometimes a word or continuous phrase is too long to fit in the available space. In such a case, use the wbr element in between words or letters to indicate where content *may* wrap if necessary to maintain legibility. To clarify, wbr does not *force* a line break like the br element; it informs the browser of an opportunity to insert a line break.

In this example, the words run together without spaces to mimic being said very quickly, and the wbrs specify points for wrapping.

Example:

```
<p>They liked to say, &quot;Friendly<wbr>Fleas<wbr>and<wbr>
Fire<wbr>Flies<wbr> Friendly<wbr>Fleas<wbr>and<wbr>Fire<wbr>
Flies<wbr>&quot; as fast as they could over and over.</p>
```

13

Embedded Content (Images, Media, and More)

One of HTML5's goals is to eliminate the need for browser plug-ins to provide media content and rich, interactive experiences. The thought is that open standards should provide all you need so you aren't bound to proprietary technologies such as Adobe Flash and Microsoft Silverlight.

To that end, media makes a huge leap in HTML5 with both native audio and video support. The latter is one of HTML5's hot-ticket items. It's also hotly debated among the browser vendors, as you'll learn in this chapter. Regardless, the likes of YouTube and Vimeo have already jumped on board, and its momentum promises to keep growing with the release of the Apple iPad and other devices that are sans plug-ins.

And, how about rich, interactive experiences? The canvas element makes huge waves in that department. This chapter doesn't have room for an in-depth exploration of canvas, but it does provide an overview and several resources so you can dig into it further on your own.

audio

Embedded audio stream

Syntax <audio></audio>

Attributes *HTML5 Only:* Global, autoplay, controls, loop, preload, src

Description

Use the audio element to embed an audio stream.

Example:

```
<audio src="ocean.oga" controls="controls">
    <!-- The HTML in here is for non-supporting user agents -->
    <p>Sorry, your browser doesn't support HTML5 audio
    with the Ogg Vorbis format. You may <a href="ocean.oga">
    ➥ download the file</a> instead.</p>
</audio>
```

The text inside the audio element is fallback content that displays only if the browser doesn't support audio. You can include a message like in Example 1, or you can include code that embeds another type of audio player, such as Flash.

 The fallback content area shouldn't be used for accessibility-focused content, such as an audio transcript.

As is the case with the video element, the major browsers have not agreed on a baseline audio format to support with the audio element, and HTML5 does not dictate one as a result. As of the time of this writing, the support was split among a few formats:

- **AAC (M4A)**: Safari 4+

- **MPEG (MP3)**: Chrome 3+, Safari 4+

- **MPEG-4 (MP4)**: Chrome 3+, Safari 4+

- **Ogg Vorbis**: Chrome 3+, Firefox 3.5+, Opera 10.5+

- **WAV**: Firefox 3.5+, Safari 4+, Opera 10.5+

Additionally, Microsoft has said that IE9 will support HTML5 audio with MP3 and AAC (M4A). You may track the latest audio support on desktop and mobile browsers at *http://www.htmlfiver.com/html5-browser-support/*.

This means you'll need to provide multiple source files to support all browsers. The source element allows you to do exactly that. Please see its entry in this chapter for an example with audio.

> **note** Even though these browsers support audio, you may experience an occasional bug. It's a pretty new feature for all of them, but it should improve over time.

Attributes in Detail

Please see the descriptions for the autoplay, controls, loop, preload, and src attributes in the video entry in this chapter, since they behave the same for audio.

canvas

Bitmap drawing surface

Syntax `<canvas></canvas>`

Attributes *HTML5 Only:* Global, `height`, `width`

Description

The canvas element is one of the headline-grabbing features of HTML5. Think of it like an entirely blank img element that you can draw on with JavaScript. It is—true to its name—a digital canvas. You can create games, graphs, animations, and other dynamic bitmap images.

Example:

```
<canvas id="piechart" width="400" height="430">
    <!-- fallback content for browsers that don't support
    canvas -->
</canvas>
```

You should always provide fallback content inside that displays if the browser doesn't support canvas or JavaScript is turned off. This content should be similar in spirit to the bitmap canvas. For instance, if the example canvas were a pie chart, your fallback content could be this:

```
<p>45% chose blue as their favorite color, 30% chose green,
and 25% chose red.</p>
```

> **note** One shortcoming of canvas is it isn't accessible. Sure, the fallback content is, but anything you draw on canvas isn't. Some proposals to remedy this are being discussed at the time of this writing.

At the time of this writing, canvas is supported by every major browser—Chrome, Firefox, Opera, Safari—except Internet Explorer. However, there are rumors (though not an announcement from Microsoft) that IE9 might include it. In the meantime, developers must resort to using ExCanvas (*http://code.google.com/p/explorercanvas/*).

Learn More

So, how do you draw on canvas? Well, you access your canvas element through its id and use the built-in JavaScript API for drawing on its surface. Unfortunately, a proper canvas drawing discussion is beyond the scope of this book, because it could fill at least a chapter by itself. But, the following resources are all you'll need to get both a sense of what you can do with canvas and how to do it:

- **Demos**: Canvas Demos (*http://www.canvasdemos.com/*) provides information and links to a wide variety of canvas applications. It also includes a tutorials section, plus a link to a cheat sheet if you search for that term.

- **Tutorials**:
    - From Mozilla: *https://developer.mozilla.org/en/Canvas_tutorial*
    - From Opera: *http://dev.opera.com/articles/view/html-5-canvas-the-basics/*
    - From Opera (advanced): *http://dev.opera.com/articles/view/blob-sallad-canvas-tag-and-javascrip/*

Attributes in Detail

- **height** and **width="*number of pixels*"**: Set the dimensions of the canvas in pixels. They default to 300 (width) and 150 (height) if undefined.

embed

Embed plug-in content

Syntax <embed> or <embed />

Attributes *HTML5 Only:* Global, height, src, type, width

Description

The embed element adds external content that requires a plug-in, such as a Flash game or movie. embed isn't part of the X/HTML specs, but browsers have supported it for years, so HTML5 has made it official.

 Please see the object element entry in Chapter 6 for differences between object and embed.

Example 1:

```
<embed src="game.swf" type="application/x-shockwave-flash"
width="500" height="500" />
```

 embed is an empty element, meaning it's properly written as <embed> or <embed /> instead of <embed></embed> and, consequently, doesn't have any inner content. However, you may need to use the invalid, latter form for backward compatibility. Also, you can't associate fallback content with embed like you can for the audio and video elements, which are not empty elements.

Even though it doesn't validate in X/HTML pages, embed is ubiquitous nowadays since it's part of the code YouTube and other video sites provide to embed a video on a site. For Example 2, I've slightly modified YouTube code (not including the object portion) in order to make it valid HTML5. Namely, I made embed an empty element and changed all ampersands to &.

Example 2:

```
<embed src="http://www.youtube.com/v/Z3ZAGBL6UBA&amp;hl=en_
US&amp;fs=1&amp;" type="application/x-shockwave-flash"
allowscriptaccess="always" allowfullscreen="true" width="480"
height="385" />
```

You'll notice two attributes, allowscriptaccess and allowfullscreen, that aren't among the four attributes native to embed. This is OK, because embed allows custom attributes specific to plug-ins. These attributes are passed into plug-ins as parameters.

Attributes in Detail

- **src="*url*"**: The path to the resource

- **type="*MIME type*"**: The MIME type of the resource, such as application/x-shockwave-flash

- **width="*number of pixels or percentage value*"** and **height="*number of pixels or percentage value*"**: The width and height in pixels or percentage values. The percentages are relative to the size of the embed's parent element.

source

A media source

Syntax <source src=""> or <source src="" />

Attributes *HTML5 Only:* Global, media, src, type

Description

Not all user agents support the same media formats for the audio and video elements, as discussed in their entries in this chapter. The source element allows you to specify multiple media source URLs for audio and video, so if the user agent doesn't support the first in the list, it looks to the second, then the third, and so on, until it finds one it does support.

Example:

```
<audio controls="controls" autoplay="autoplay">
    <!-- UA looks at this first -->
    <source src="laughter.oga" type="audio/ogg;
    ➥ codecs=vorbis" />
    <!-- then this, etc. -->
    <source src="laughter.spx" type="audio/ogg;
    ➥ codecs=speex" />
</audio>
```

This is the recommended practice since you'll risk shutting out users if you provide only one source. Note that you are permitted to use source only in either an audio or video element. Please see an example of source with the video element in the video entry in this chapter.

Attributes in Detail

- media="*media query list*": If desired, specify the media platform(s), such as screen or projection, to help the browser determine whether it'll be useful to load the resource specified by src. If you omit the media attribute, which is common, it defaults to all. See the link element in Chapter 3 for more information.

- src="*uri*": *Required*. This is the path to the media resource.

- type="*MIME type*": This specifies the type of the media resource (for example, audio/mp3, video/ogg, or video/mp4) specified by src to help the user agent determine whether it supports it. The optional codecs parameter serves the same purpose but is specific to the codec(s) used to encode the media. In both cases, if the user agent knows it doesn't support it, it looks at the next source, if any. type must be a valid MIME type. You'll find several examples of type and codecs configurations for both audio and video at *http://www.whatwg.org/specs/web-apps/current-work/multipage/video.html#the-source-element*.

video

An embedded video

Syntax <video></video>

Attributes *HTML5 Only:* Global, autoplay, controls, height, loop, poster, preload, src, width

Description

Native video playback is one of HTML5's highest-profile additions, and it's implemented with the video element.

Example 1 (basic video embed):

```
<video src="your-video.ogv" controls="controls">
    <!-- The HTML in here is for non-supporting user
    agents -->
</video>
```

Adding a video to your page is that easy—no plug-ins, complicated embedding methods, or JavaScript required. src is the path to your video, and controls="controls" (or simply controls, if you prefer that format) makes default play, pause, and other buttons available to the user. (See "Attributes in Detail" regarding other attributes.) Or you can create your own controls and add behavior with JavaScript (see *https://developer.mozilla.org/En/Using_audio_and_video_in_Firefox* for a taste).

The HTML inside `video` is optional though highly encouraged. It displays only if the browser doesn't support the `video` element. Typically, you'll want to include an embed method for another video player format, such as Flash, or perhaps a simple message with a link directly to the video file for offline viewing. Please see Example 2 and related content for the best way to approach fallback solutions.

note Do not use `video`'s inner content for accessibility means, such as to include a transcript of the video. In theory, the video itself should be encoded with captions or related information. At the time of this writing, there wasn't a standard captioning format for the `video` element, but discussions were underway.

The `video` Format Debate

Adding `video` may be simple, but unfortunately, it's been difficult to get the major browser vendors to agree upon the baseline standard video format. It's been a hotly debated issue, the details of which I won't get into here, though you can read a summary at *http://lists.whatwg.org/htdig.cgi/whatwg-whatwg.org/2009-June/020620.html*. As a result, HTML5 removed an initial requirement that user agents must support Ogg Theora at a minimum and now doesn't require a specific format.

Currently, the following formats work with the `video` element on the browsers listed:

- **Ogg Theora**: Universal support for an open, licensing- and royalty-free format such as Ogg Theora is the Holy Grail, but the issue isn't quite that simple. The supporting browsers are Chrome 3.0+, Firefox 3.5+, and Opera 10.5+.

- **H.264**: The popular format in which vast amounts (for example, YouTube et al.) of video content is already encoded. The supporting browsers are Chrome 3.0+, Safari 3.1+, and Internet Explorer with Google Chrome Frame installed. Internet Explorer 9, still in development at the time of this writing, will support H.264 (without the need for Google Chrome Frame).

> **tip** You may track the latest support for video on desktop and mobile browsers at *http://www.htmlfiver.com/html5-browser-support/*.

As you can see, neither format is supported across the range of browsers. Therefore, unless you know your audience primarily uses one of these sets of browsers—very unlikely, except for narrower platforms like the iPhone and iPad—you'll need to encode your video in at least two formats.

That's not particularly convenient, but suppose you do generate two versions. How do you serve them to users? The source element has you covered.

Multiple Media Sources with the source Element

Example 2 shows how to use the source element to specify multiple media sources.

Example 2 (provide multiple video sources):

```
<video controls="controls">
    <!-- option 1: OGG Theora video and Vorbis audio -->
    <source src="your-video.ogv" type='video/ogg;
    ➥codecs="theora, vorbis"' />
    <!-- option 2: H.264 -->
    <source src="your-video.mp4" type='video/mp4;
    ➥codecs="avc1.42E01E, mp4a.40.2"' />
    <!-- The HTML below here is for non-supporting user
    agents, for example, you could embed a Flash video
    player. -->
      . . .
</video>
```

Note that you specify the src on each source element instead of on the video start tag. The user agent checks the type and codecs information of the first source to see whether it supports it. If it knows it doesn't, it moves to the next one, and so on. Please see the source element in this chapter for more details.

tip Video for Everybody (*http://camendesign.com/code/video_for_ everybody*) is a block of code (no JavaScript required) you may use that leverages the video and source elements with fallbacks for QuickTime and Flash so your video can work on all browsers, provided your video is encoded in the variety of formats.

Attributes in Detail

- autoplay: If present, this Boolean attribute instructs the user agent to start playing the media when the page loads, rather than waiting for the user to initiate playback. Here's an example of using it: <video src="skywriter.ogg" autoplay="autoplay"></video> (or simply, autoplay).

- controls: If present, this Boolean attribute instructs the user agent to display controls so the user can control playback. These default controls include play, pause, volume, seek, and in some instances more (browsers are supposed to provide more, but not all do). The look and feel of the default controls varies between supported browsers. If you create your own controls with JavaScript, the default controls show if scripting is disabled.

- loop: If present, this Boolean attribute instructs the user agent to play the media again when it reaches the end.

- poster="*url*": If present, this is the path to an image that is intended to be representative of the video, such as one of the initial frames. HTML5 recommends browsers show the poster frame when the video isn't available (such as when loading), though they may choose to show nothing instead. User agents have full discretion of what to show when the video is paused on the first frame.

- `preload="none|metadata|auto"`: Preloaded video loads in part or full before the user initiates playback. The `preload` attribute is your means to suggest to the user agent what you think will result in the best user experience regarding preloading. It's just a hint; the user agent may choose to ignore your setting if, for example, bandwidth is not a concern. `preload` has no effect if `autoplay` is present. The options are as follows:

  - `preload="none"`: This suggests that it isn't necessary to preload the video or any metadata. Use this if it's less likely the user will play the video or if you want to minimize server traffic.

  - `preload="metadata"`: This is the same as `none` except to hint that fetching video metadata only (not the video itself), such as the dimensions, duration, and so on, is OK.

  - `preload="auto"`: This hints to the user agent that server traffic is not a concern so it may preload some or all of the video.

- `src="url"`: This is the path to the video.

- `width="number of pixels or percentage value"` and `height="number of pixels or percentage value"`: These define the width and height of the video. If they don't equal the dimensions of the video's intrinsic size, the video will shrink or stretch accordingly and may be letterboxed or pillarboxed. Note that the video will maintain its native aspect ratio regardless of whether `width` and `height` reflect that aspect ratio. If the `width` and `height` are undefined, the player typically renders at the intrinsic size of the video. You may define these with CSS instead, such as with `video { width: 320px; height: 240px; }`.

14

Forms

Forms make a big leap in HTML5 as part of its focus on making Web applications richer and their development easier.

Among the most compelling additions are the input types for color and date pickers, numbers, a range slider, search, email and telephone number fields, and more. Plus, there are attributes for marking fields as required, or specifying a regular expression that performs pattern matching without JavaScript. Please see the "HTML5 and the input Element" box in Chapter 7's input entry for more information.

HTML5 also includes new form-related *elements*, which this chapter covers.

(Note: Please also see the meter and progress elements in Chapter 12 since you may find them valuable to use with a form.)

datalist

A list of predefined options

Syntax `<datalist>`

      `<option></option>`

      `. . .`

   `</datalist>`

Attributes *HTML5 Only:* Global

Description

The `datalist` element specifies a list of predefined `option` elements for an `input` element. For instance, you may turn a text `input` control into a combo box, meaning the user may either type in a value or choose from the `datalist`'s `options`. Setting the `input`'s `list` attribute to the `datalist`'s `id` hooks them together.

If a browser supports `datalist`, it doesn't display any of its contents, except that it makes the `options` available once the user interacts with the `input`. This allows you to add fallback content in the `datalist` content for browsers that don't support `datalist`. (There's one notable exception: As of this writing, Chrome doesn't show the fallback content even though it doesn't support `datalist`.)

In this example, I predefine some drink `options`. Users may choose from those or type something like *Tang*, if that's their preference. For the purposes of being really explicit to demonstrate the concept, I included "fallback" in the attribute values of each element that is ignored by a browser that supports `datalist`. (Note: The example assumes the code is in a `form` element.)

Example:

```
<label for="drink">Enter your favorite drink:</label>
<input type="text" name="drink" id="drink" list="drinkslist">
<datalist id="drinkslist">
    <label for="drinkfallback">Or, select a drink from this
    list:</label>
    <select name="drinkfallback" id="drinkfallback">
    <!-- the options are not ignored, just the select -->
        <option value="apple juice">apple juice</option>
        <option value="frappe">frappe</option>
        <option value="water">water</option>
    </select>
</datalist>
```

Technically, you shouldn't have to specify the value attributes on the options, but Opera 9+, the only browser to provide reasonable (though incomplete) support for datalist at the time of this writing, doesn't present an option's inner text, only the value (and the label attribute value if value is present). You can't leave out the inner text, though, because an empty select box would display as the fallback content.

Here's how the example looks in a browser that *doesn't* support datalist. (I added a little CSS to make it wrap and breathe a bit.)

Until Opera or another browser has complete support for datalist, Section 2.1 of *http://docs.google.com/View?id=dch3zh37_0cf8kc8c4* illustrates how a proper implementation might look and behave.

keygen

A key pair generator control

Syntax `<keygen name="">` or `<keygen name="" />`

Attributes *HTML5 Only:* Global, autofocus, challenge, disabled, form, keytype, name

Description

The keygen element is a key pair generator control. When the form is submitted, "the private key is stored in the local keystore, and the public key is packaged and sent to the server." Many browsers (but not Internet Explorer) have supported keygen for a long time even though it was never an official element in any HTML spec. HTML5 makes it official.

Example:

```
<form action="processkey.php" method="post"
enctype="multipart/form-data">
    <div>
        <label for="key">Choose a Key Grade:</label>
        <keygen name="key" id="key">
        <input type="submit" value="Submit Key">
    </div>
</form>
```

keygen renders like a select box in supporting browsers, though its options may be different. This shows how keygen renders in Chrome:

Choose a Key Grade: | 2048 (High Grade) ▼ | Submit key...

HTML5 doesn't dictate how the generated private key should be used, though presumably, it could result in a client certificate being generated by the server and offered to the user for the purposes of SSL and certificate authentication services.

Attributes in Detail

- **autofocus**: When present, this Boolean attribute tells the browser to set focus on the keygen control as soon as the page is loaded. This allows users to use the control without having to tab to it or click it first.

- **challenge="*challenge string*"**: When present, the value is packaged with the submitted key.

- **disabled**: When present, this Boolean attribute disables the element so the user can't interact with it. Furthermore, a disabled control doesn't receive focus, it is skipped in tabbing navigation, and its value is not submitted with the form.

- **form="*form id*"**: By default, each form control is associated with its nearest ancestor form element (that is, the form that contains it). Set this attribute to the id of a different form in the page to override this behavior.

- **keytype="*keyword*"**: rsa is the default keyword that supporting browsers understand. Firefox also supports ec, and both Firefox and Safari support dsa. If keytype="rsa", the state of the key is RSA. User agents are not required to support this or other values, only "recognize values whose corresponding algorithms they support."

- **name**: This assigns a name to the keygen for processing the form.

output

The result of a calculation

Syntax <output>

Attributes *HTML5 Only:* Global, for, form, name

Description

The output element represents the results of a calculation.

Example:

```
<form action="calculate-it.php" method="post">
    <input name="value1" id="value1" type="number"> x
    <input name="value2" id="value2" type="number"> =
    <output name="total" for="value1 value2"></output>
    <input name="submit" type="submit">
</form>
```

One application of output could be a shopping cart that updates the total price as the user changes the number of products or the shipping option. As an enhancement for users whose browsers support JavaScript, you could also process output calculations on the client side by wiring a JavaScript function to update the output every time a change is made to the cart. That's not a replacement for server-side processing, though, since you don't want to shut out users with JavaScript disabled.

Attributes in Detail

- **for="*control id(s)*"**: This explicitly associates the output with each control involved in the calculation when it is set to a space-separated list of the control ids. The controls may exist anywhere in the same document. Please see the example.

- **form="*form id*"**: By default, an output is associated with its nearest ancestor form element (that is, the form that contains it). Set this attribute to the id of a different form in the page to override this behavior.

- **name="*output name*"**: This assigns a name to the output for the purposes of processing the form.

Interactive Elements

HTML5 includes two new interactive elements, details and menu, and their supporting elements, summary and command, respectively. They support one of HTML5's goals of making Web application development easier, richer, and more accessible by building features into native HTML elements.

This chapter explains how to leverage them to create application-style toolbars and contextual menus (in the case of menu), as well as expandable and collapsible information and form control modules (in the case of details). Please be aware, though, that much of the native functionality that these elements promise doesn't exist in any major browser at the time of this writing. That is expected to change as browsers continue to incorporate more and more of HTML5's features. Like the other HTML5 chapters, this one details how the elements and attribute should behave once implemented correctly.

> **note** The device element is not included, since it's considered an addition to HTML beyond HTML5 and its details were still being defined at the time of this writing. You may track its progress at *http://dev.w3.org/html5/html-device/*. In short, device "represents a device selector, to allow the user to give the page access to a device, for example a video camera" for videoconferencing from HTML applications.

command

A menu command

Syntax <command label=""> or <command label="" />

Attributes *HTML5 Only:* Global, checked, disabled, icon, label, radiogroup, type

Description

The command element represents a choice within a menu element. A command may be one of three states, as specified by its type attribute. The default is a normal command (type="command" or no type) that is associated with an action (see the example in the menu entry in this chapter). Another is a toggle (type="radio"), as shown in the following example. The third state is a choice of one item from a list of items (type="checkbox").

Suppose you write a word processing Web application, and you want to provide a context menu so users can easily toggle the track changes option from where they are typing, rather than navigating through the toolbar at the top.

Example (context menu with radio commands):

```
<menu type="context" id="trackChanges">
    <h1>Track Changes</h1>
    <command type="radio" radiogroup="tracking" label="On" />
    <command type="radio" radiogroup="tracking" label="Off" />
</menu>
<article contenteditable="true" contextmenu="trackChanges">
    . . . [paragraphs and other content the user may edit] . . .
</article>
```

The radiogroup specifies a name for the group of related radio commands that toggle when the command is toggled (in other words, the selected one is toggled on, and all others in the radiogroup are toggled off). The contextmenu attribute on the article element is set to the menu's id in order to specify the menu as the article's context menu; users may not access it outside the article.

A type="checkbox" command may be structured similarly but would not include the radiogroup attribute.

note You may use menu in other ways besides a context menu. Please see the menu entry in this chapter for an explanation of menu types, as well as another example and further discussion of command, including how to make a command functional.

Attributes in Detail

- **checked**: If present, this Boolean attribute indicates the command is selected. It's permitted only if type is set to checkbox or radio.

- **disabled**: If present, this Boolean attribute makes the command unavailable, though it may still display.

- `icon="`*image URL*`"`: This specifies the location of an image that represents the command and is shown to the user.

- `label="`*text*`"`: *Required.* This specifies the command name text that is shown to the user.

- `radiogroup="`*name*`"`: This value is a name of your choosing and may be assigned only if `type="radio"`. Please see the description in this entry.

- `type="checkbox|command|radio"`: This defines a command's state. The command defaults to `type="command"` if type is omitted. Please see the description in this entry.

details

An expandable widget

Syntax `<details></details>`

Attributes *HTML5 Only:* Global, open

Description

The `details` element expands or collapses to reveal or hide information or controls. JavaScript isn't required for this behavior, since it's built into the element.

By default, a `details` element should render as closed, so its content doesn't display except for the `summary` element (the open attribute sets it to open instead). `summary` is the caption for the content and, depending on the user agent, may be the means by which the user can open or close the `details`. If `summary` is absent, the user agent should display a term of its choosing, such as *Details*.

These following examples show a couple ways you might use details.
The first is a football (American-style) game tracker. The summary provides
a snapshot of the action, and the user can learn more by opening the
details element. It could even have a video element in it. The second
example is a list of emoticons the user could toggle open in a chat application and then close after selecting one.

Examples:

```
<details>
    <summary>Good Guys 20, Bad Guys 17, fourth quarter
    ➥</summary>
    <!-- Code showing score by quarter and
        other statistics would go here. -->
</details>

<details>
    <summary>Emoticons</summary>
    <ul>
        <li><a href="#"><img src="icon/super_smiley.png"
        width="20" height="20" alt="Super smiley" /></a></li>
        <li><a href="#"><img src="icon/guffaw.png" width="20"
        height="20" alt="Guffaw" /></a></li>
        . . . [more emoticons] . . .
    </ul>
</details>
```

Another application of details could build on the drawing tool example
from the menu entry in this chapter. A floating palette like those in
Photoshop could include a series of stacked details elements that reveal
form inputs to type in shape dimensions or pick a color, and so on.

Try to craft a summary that reflects the values of the details whenever possible. The football example demonstrates this.

Attributes in Detail

■ **open**: When present, this Boolean attribute specifies that the content within details should be shown to the user. User agents shouldn't show it by default except the summary.

menu

An application menu

Syntax <menu></menu>

Attributes *HTML5 Only:* Global, label, type

Description

The menu element has had a previous life in HTML, but it's deprecated in X/HTML. HTML5 both resurrects and refines it to add value.

A menu may be a context menu or a toolbar, as specified by its type attribute (it's neither if type is undefined, as shown in the example). A *context menu* is like the kind that displays in software when you right-click or Option-click (or Alt-click in some cases). A *toolbar* is like the kind available along the top of most software (though a toolbar menu won't necessarily appear at the top). In each case, a menu has one or more choices.

 menu is appropriate for Web application menus, not navigation. Please see the nav element in Chapter 11 regarding structuring navigation.

The command element is one way to define your menu's options. (Please see its entry in this chapter for more details.)

Example (toolbar menu with commands):

```
<menu type="toolbar">
    <li>
        <menu label="File">
            <command label="New" icon="icon/new.png"
title="Start a new    drawing" />
            <command label="Open" icon="icon/open.png"
title="Open a    drawing" />
            <command label="Save" icon="icon/save.png"
title="Save your drawing" disabled="disabled" />
            . . . [more commands] . . .
        </menu>
    </li>
    <li>
        <menu label="Edit">
            . . . [commands for Edit menu] . . .
        </menu>
    </li>
</menu>
```

This example shows a menu of type="toolbar" for an imaginary drawing app (using the canvas element, for instance). It assumes the user's browser has JavaScript enabled, since you can't apply behavior to command elements (or canvas, for that matter) without it. Note that the type is specified only on the parent menu since the nested menus are part of the toolbar (a menu doesn't require nested menus, however). In the example, each nested menu is represented in the interface by its label attribute (although as of this writing, no popular user agent renders it yet).

> **note** The use of li without an ol or ul element parent is particular to menu. menu allows nearly all other HTML elements, too, though you can't structure some of it with li elements and the rest with something else.

The disabled attribute renders the Save command element inactive. Presumably, you would remove disabled programmatically to enable the command once the user performs a change, as is common in applications. The title attribute text may display as a tooltip as the pointer hovers over the command; it is optional, like the icon attribute.

A command element doesn't perform an action unless you specify its behavior via an onclick event. For instance, selecting the New command could call a JavaScript function that starts a new drawing. I strongly recommend you add the onclick events unobtrusively rather than as inline onclick attributes. (Please search for *unobtrusive JavaScript* online for details.)

Previously, I noted that command is just one way to represent a menu's choices. You may also use elements such as a, button, and select. If you were to use button, the example's structure would be the same except button elements would replace the commands. This approach could be friendlier to browsers that don't support command, because they would still be able to display the list of buttons.

Context Menus

A context menu is structured the same as a toolbar except it has a type="context" declaration. You associate a context menu with another element by setting the element's contextmenu attribute value to the menu's id. Please see the example in the command entry in this chapter.

> **note** Use the hr element as a separator within a menu as needed.

note   HTML5 suggests how a menu may appear but doesn't define it outright, so user agent renderings may vary.

Attributes in Detail

- **type="context|toolbar"**: Defines a menu as either a context menu or a toolbar. If type is unspecified, the menu is a list of options that's neither type. For instance, the nested menu in the example doesn't have a type since it's a submenu.

- **label="*text*"**: The menu's label that is shown to the user.

summary

Details summary or caption

Syntax <summary></summary>

Attributes *HTML5 Only:* Global

Description

The summary element provides a summary, caption, or legend for the other contents of a details element. Please see the details entry in this chapter for more information.

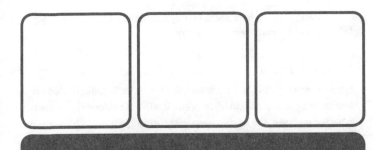

Appendix: Alphabetical HTML Elements Page Listing

LEGEND:

(*HTML5 only*) HTML 4 and XHTML 1 include all elements except those marked with (*HTML5 only*), which are unique to HTML5.

* HTML5 includes all elements except those marked with an asterisk (*).

Index

Meet Creative Edge.

A new resource of unlimited books, videos and tutorials for creatives from the world's leading experts.

Creative Edge is your one stop for inspiration, answers to technical questions and ways to stay at the top of your game so you can focus on what you do best—being creative.

All for only $24.99 per month for access—any day any time you need it.